Real World

Colouring Book

For Advanced Users & Adults

50 Images

**Created From Real Life Photos
For You To Colour As You Please.**

ISBN 978-0-359-82275-1
90000
9 780359 822751

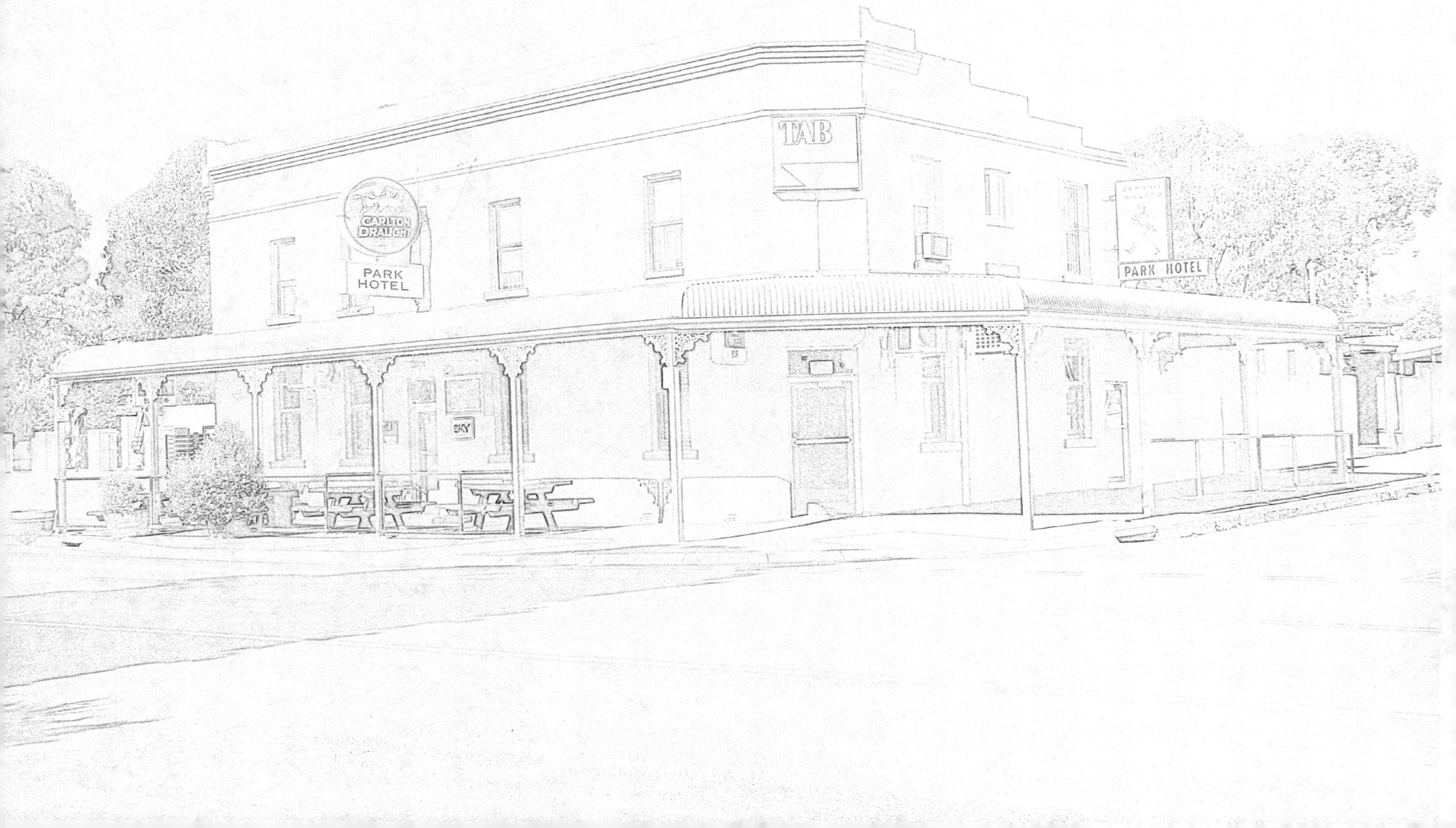
CARLTON DRAUGHT
PARK HOTEL
SKY
TAB
PARK HOTEL

185

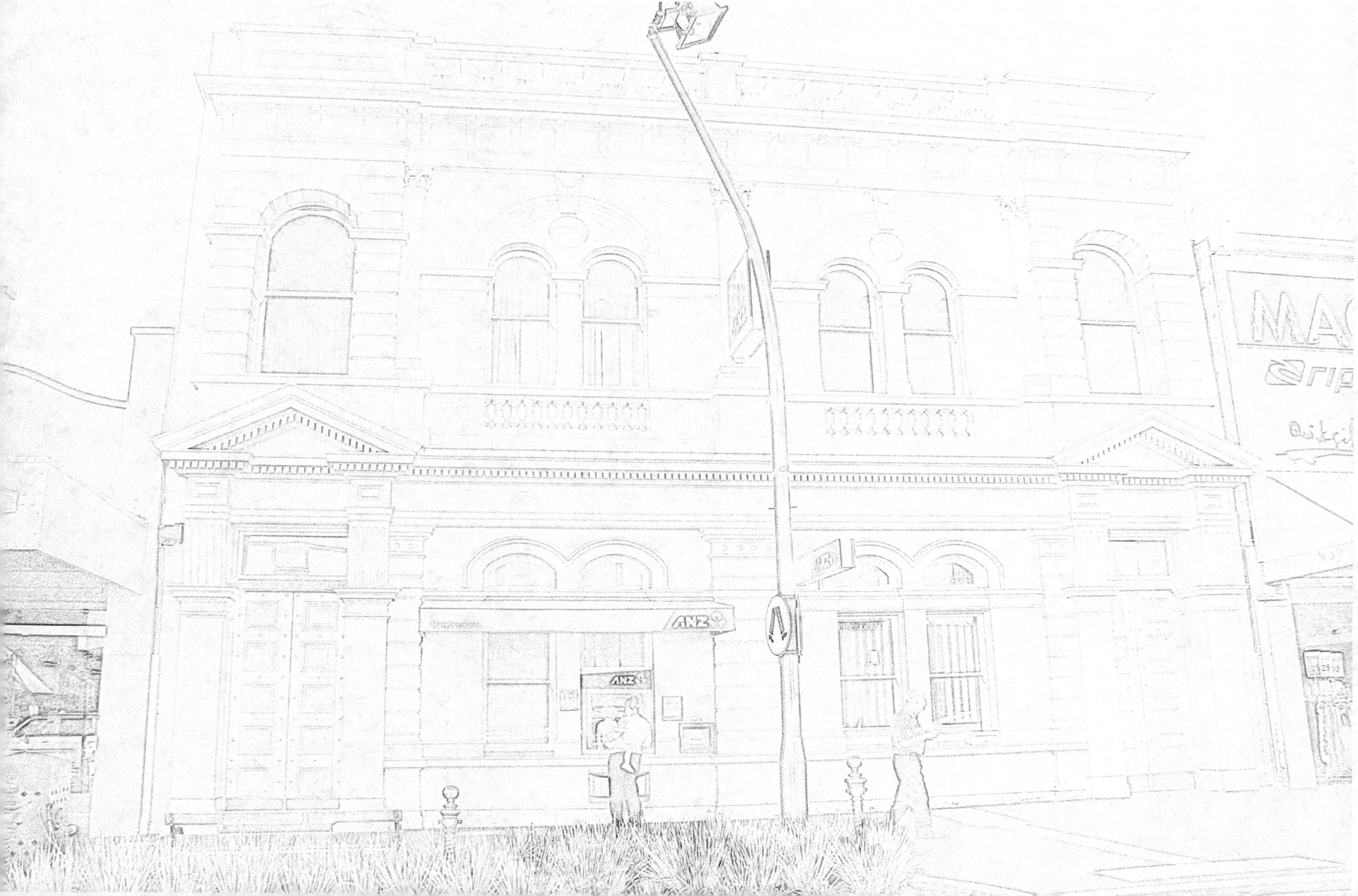
ANZ

MARYBOROUGH POST OFFICE

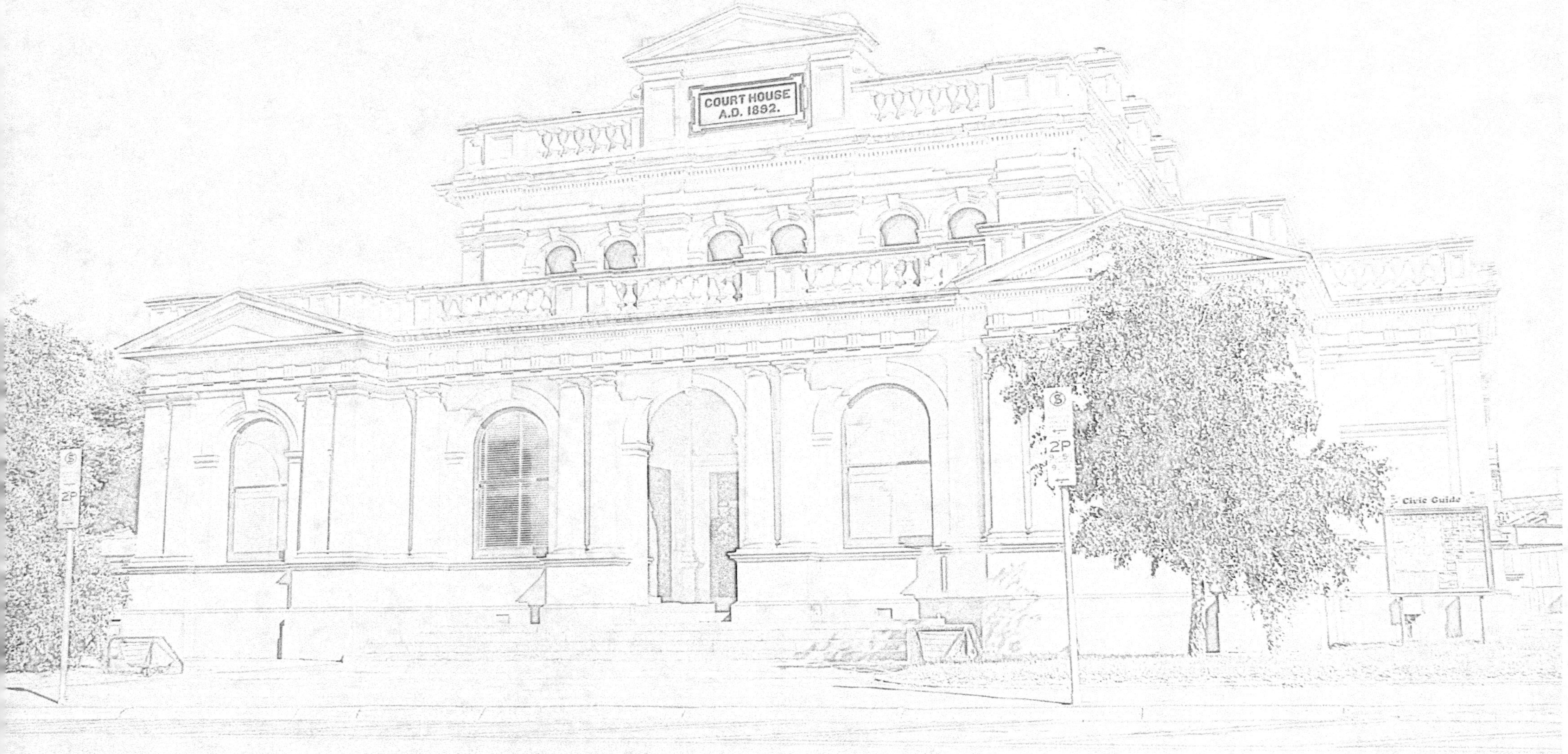
COURT HOUSE
A.D. 1892.
2P
2P
Civic Guide

CENTRAL GOLDFIELDS
ART GALLERY

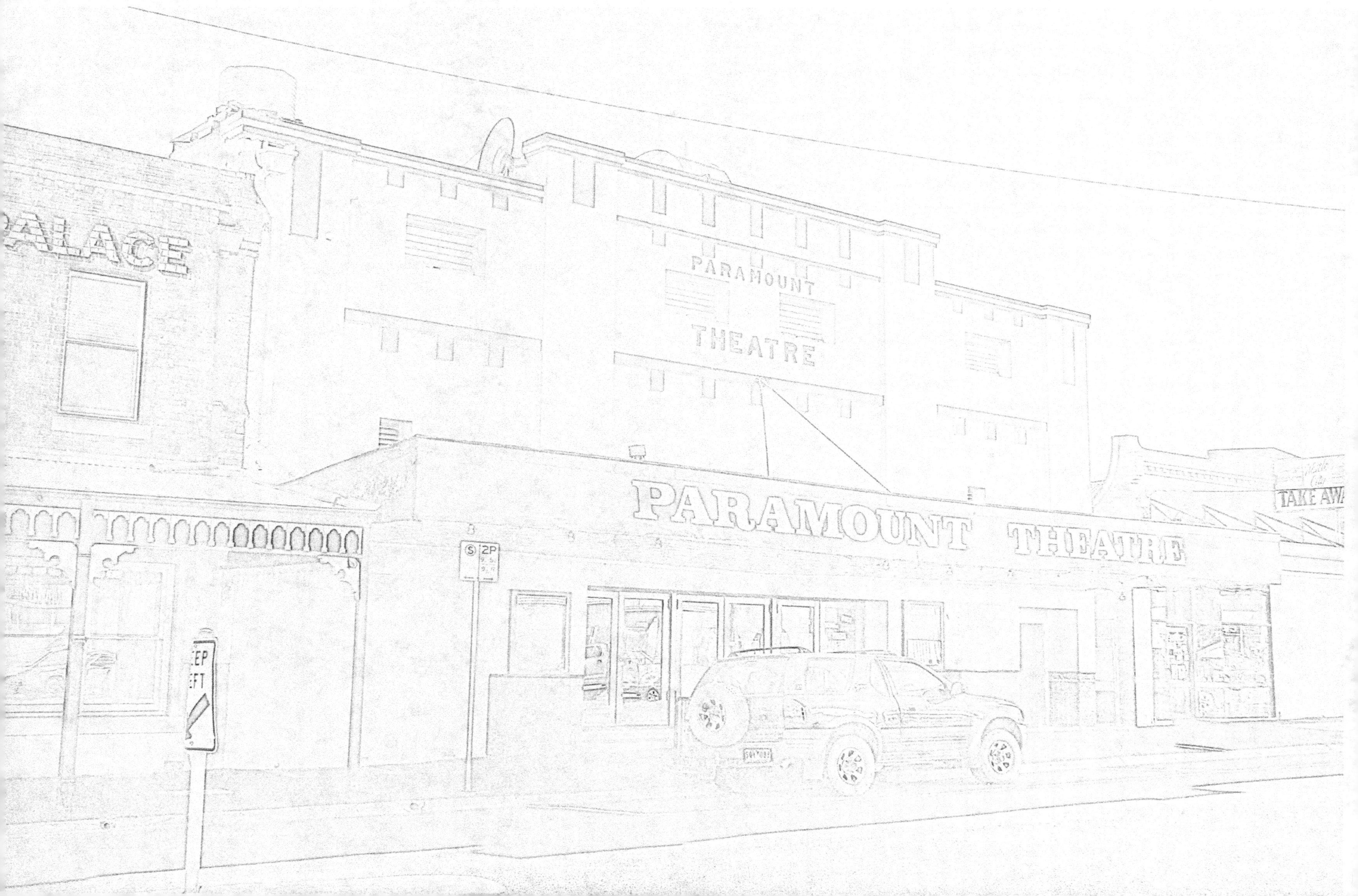
PARAMOUNT
THEATRE
PARAMOUNT THEATRE
TAKE AWA
2P

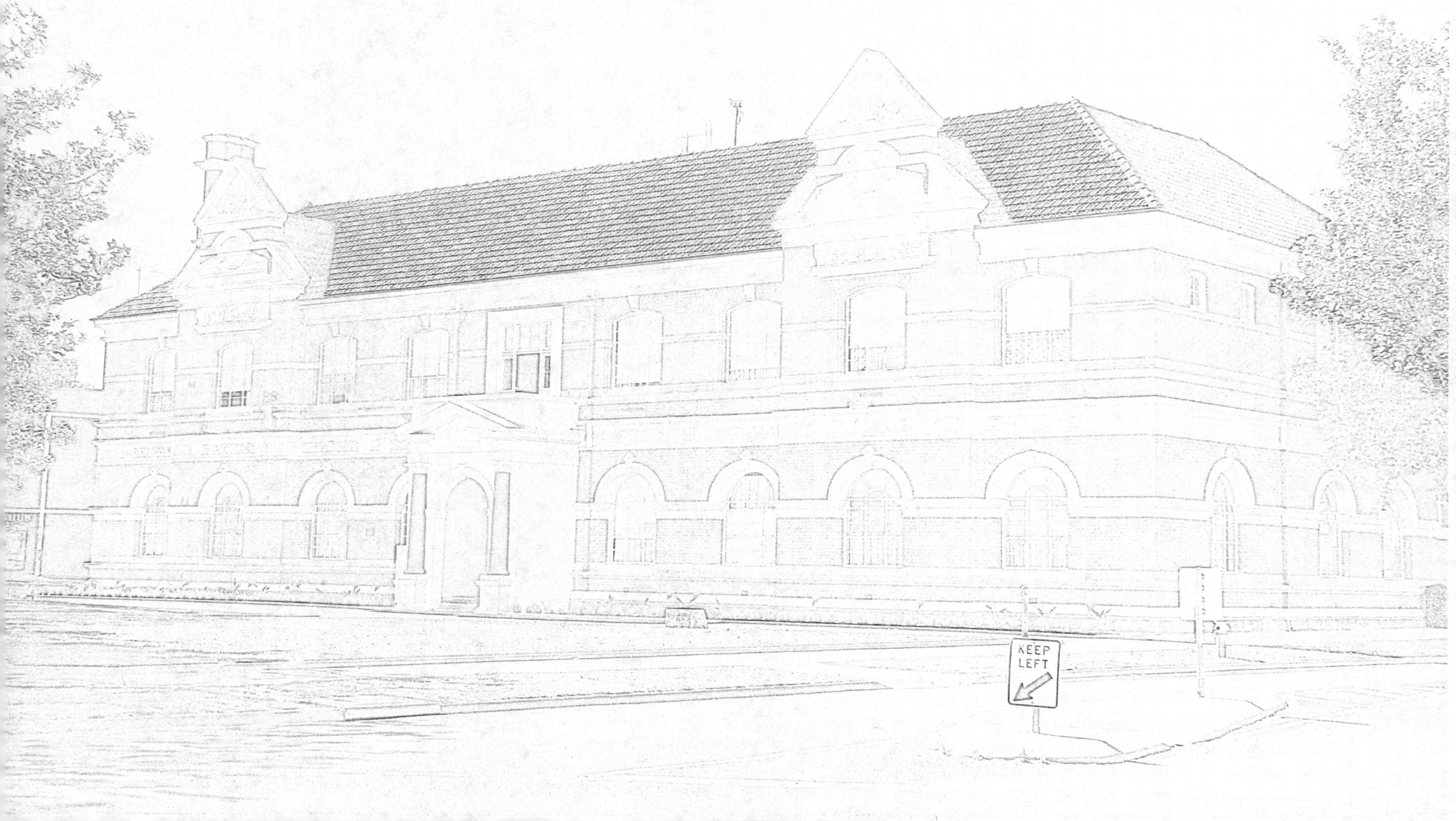
KEEP LEFT

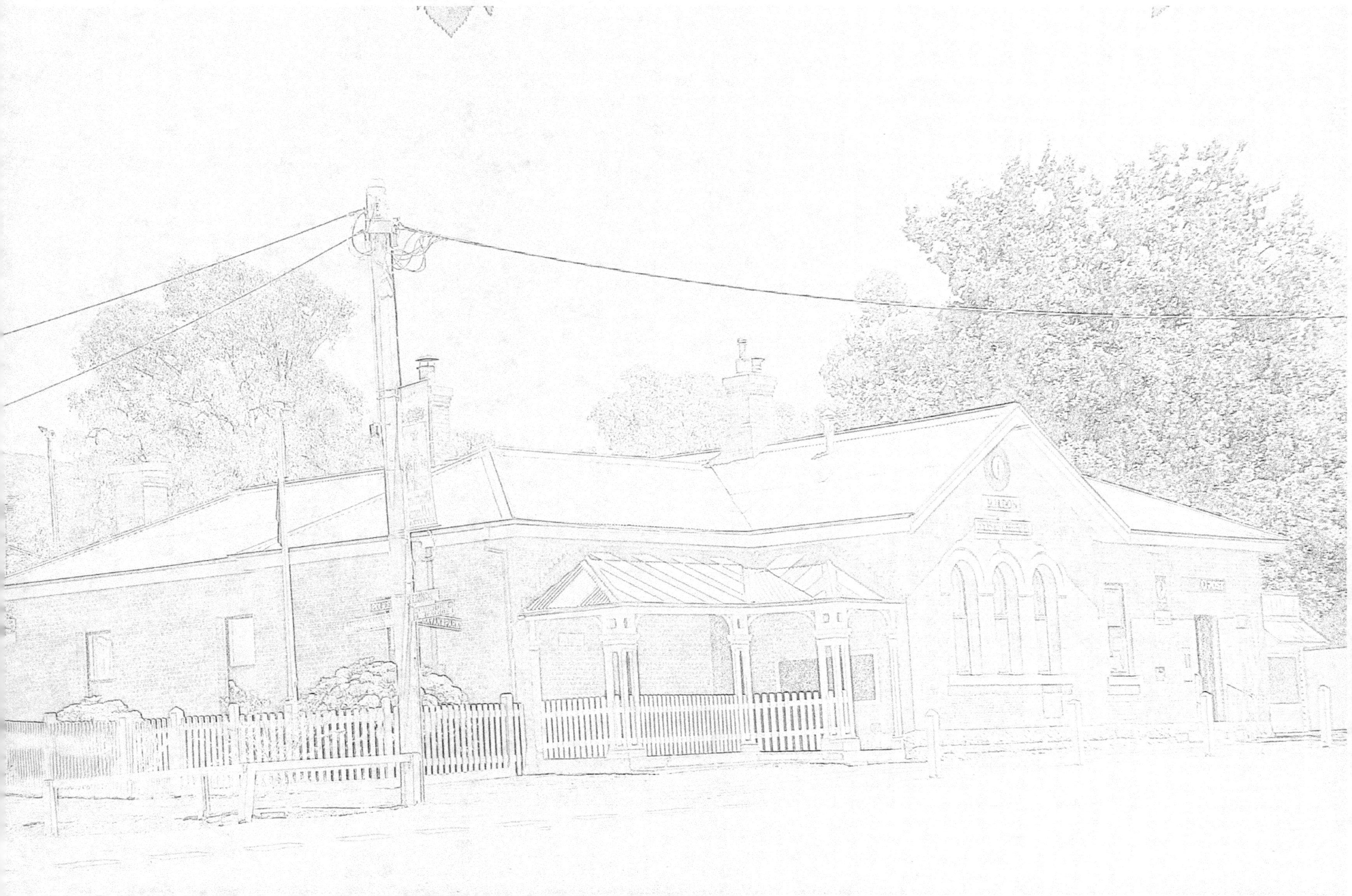

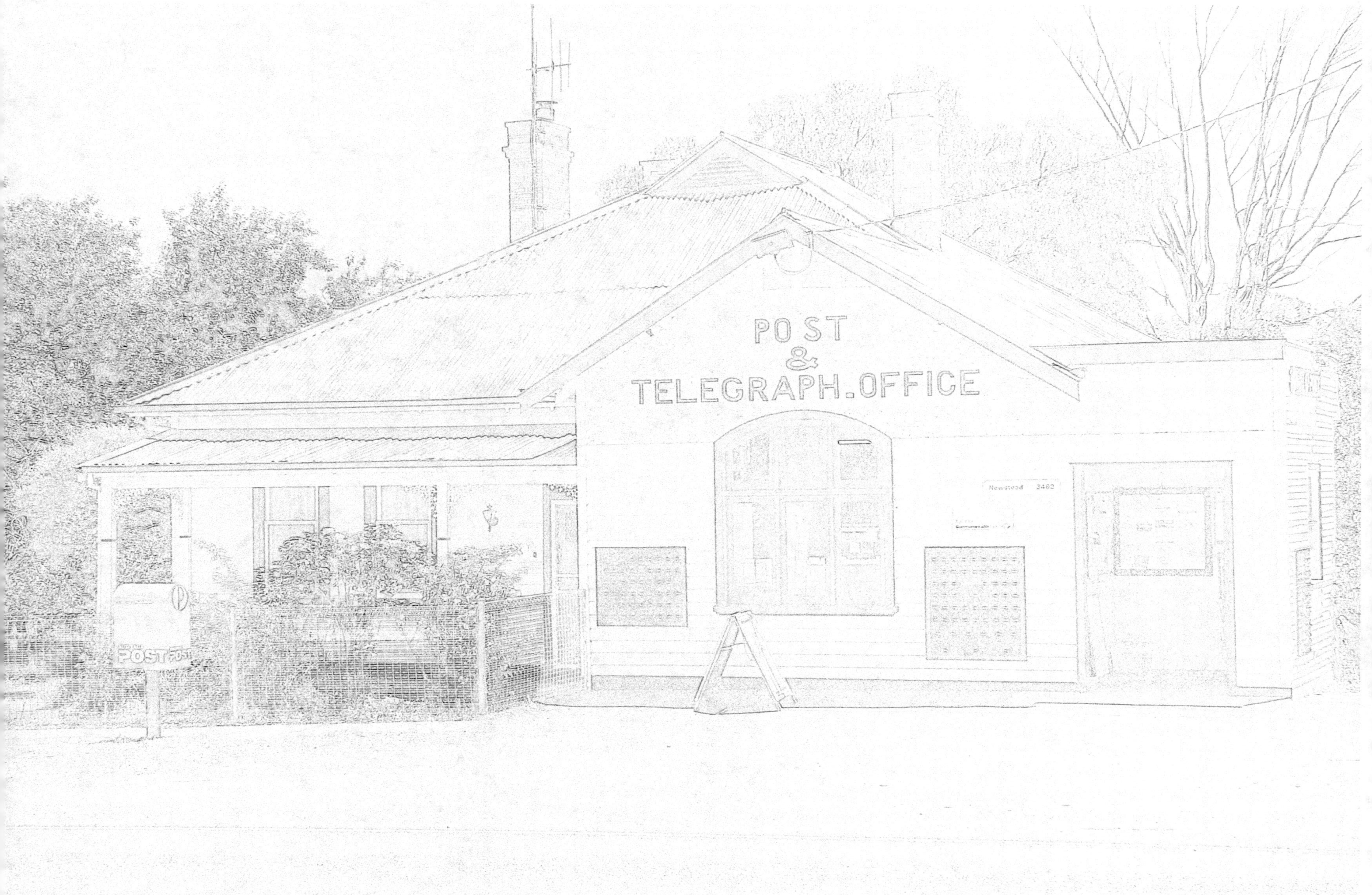

POST
&
TELEGRAPH. OFFICE
Newstead 3462
POST

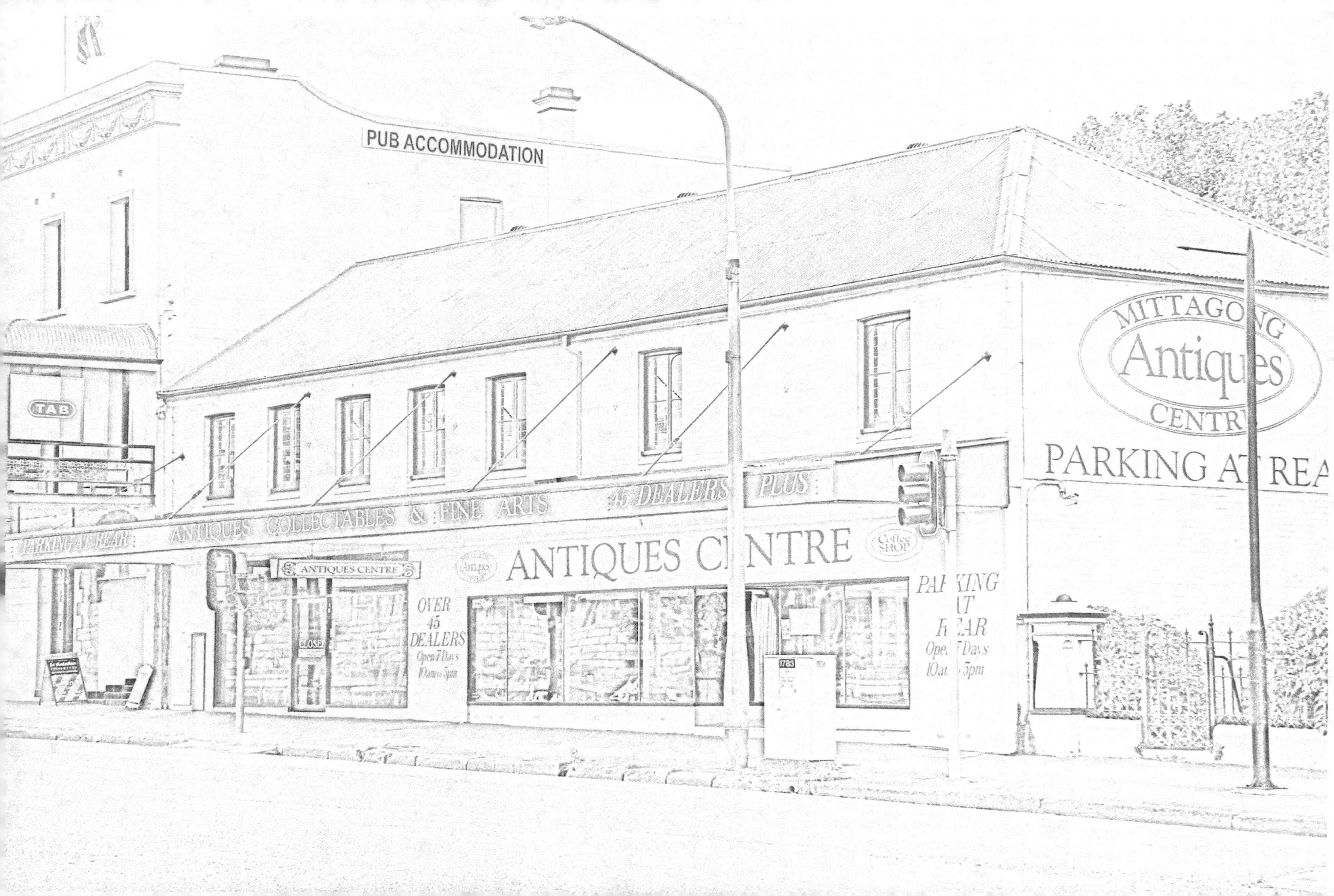
PUB ACCOMMODATION
TAB
PARKING AT REAR
ANTIQUES COLLECTABLES & FINE ARTS
45 DEALERS PLUS
ANTIQUES CENTRE
ANTIQUES C NTRE
Coffee SHOP
CLOSED
OVER 45 DEALERS Open 7 Days 10am to 5pm
MITTAGONG Antiques CENTRE
PARKING AT REA

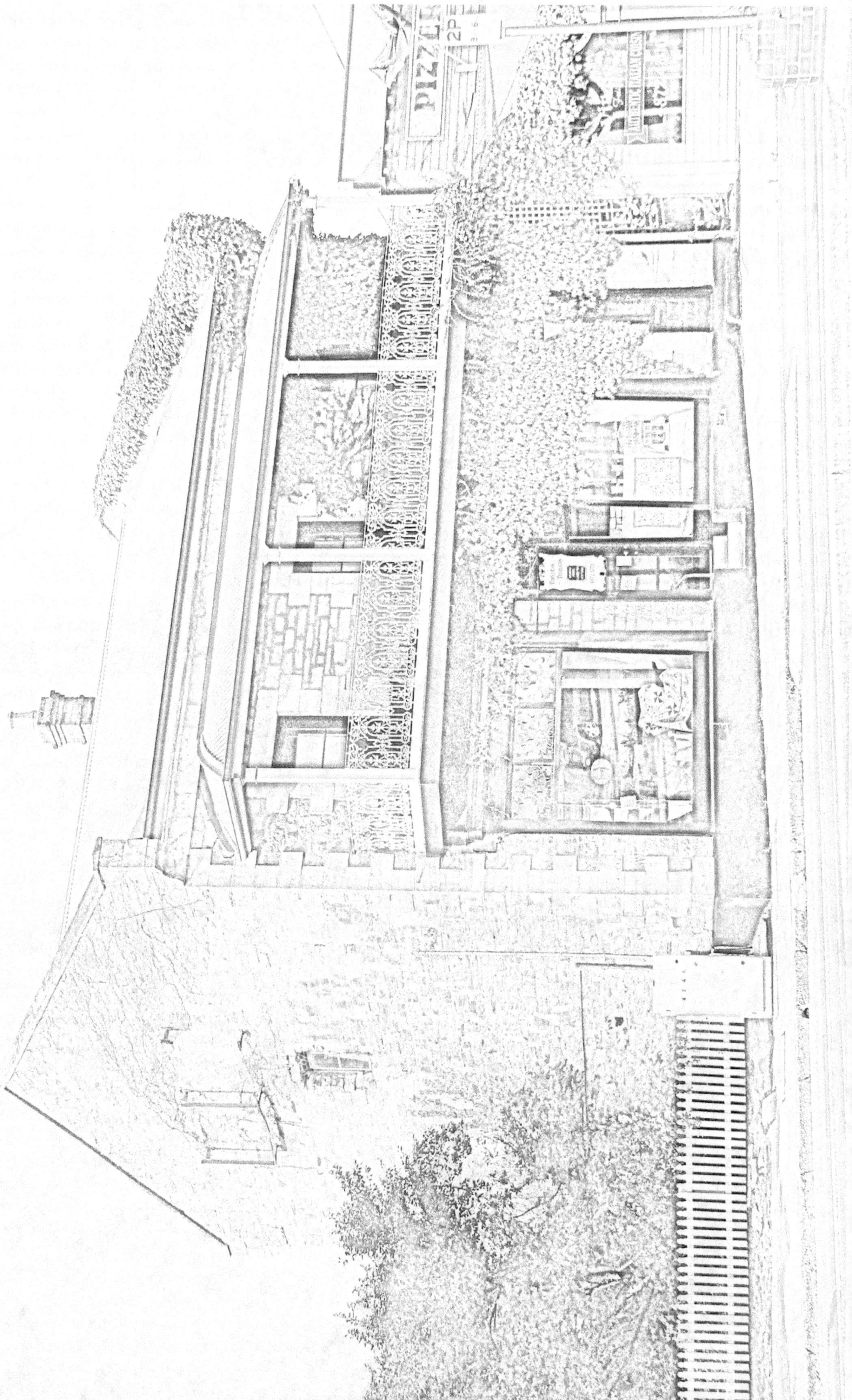

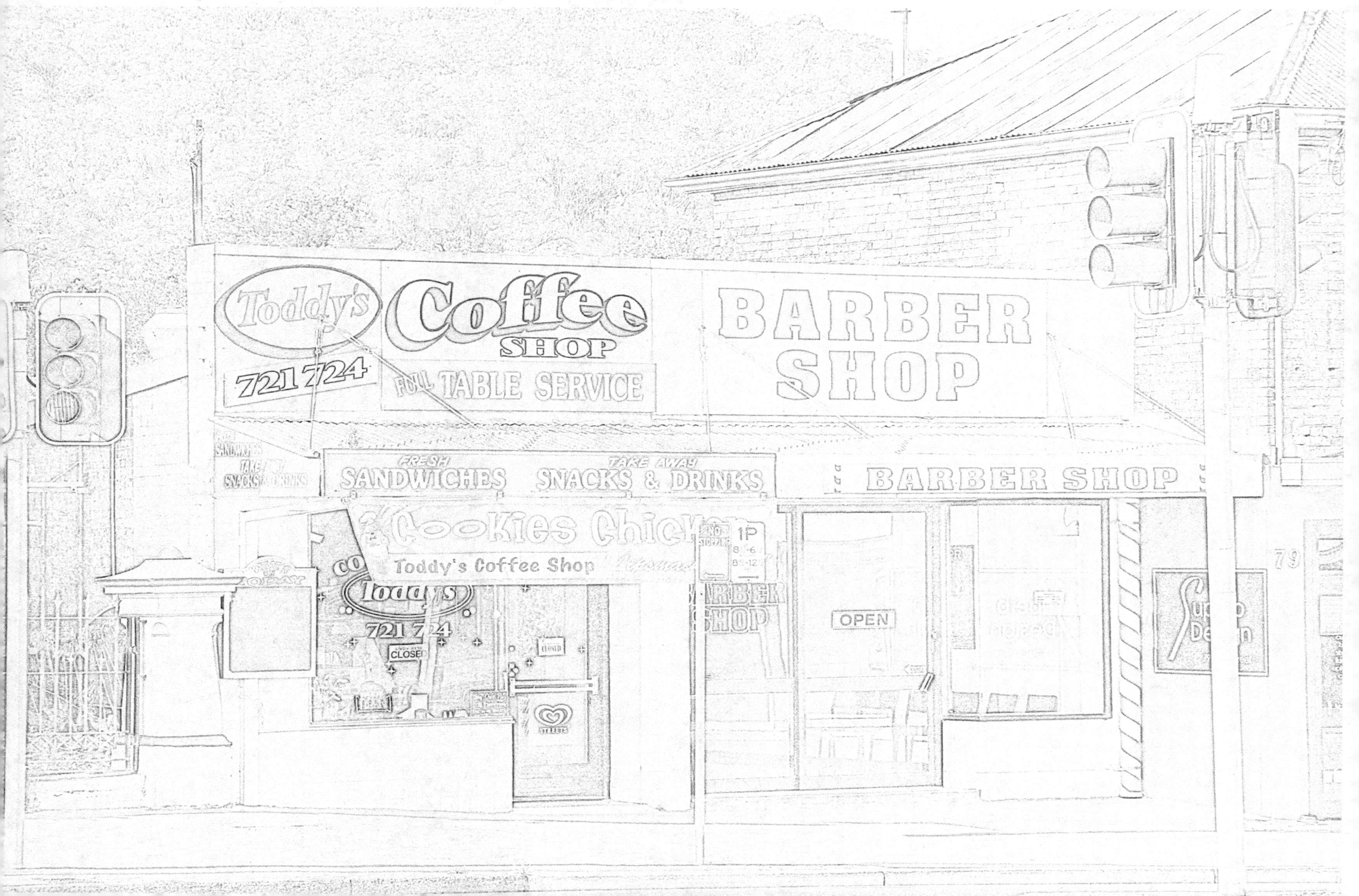
Toddy's Coffee SHOP
721 724
FULL TABLE SERVICE
BARBER SHOP
FRESH SANDWICHES
TAKE AWAY SNACKS & DRINKS
BARBER SHOP
Toddy's Coffee Shop
1P
OPEN
CLOSED
721 724
79

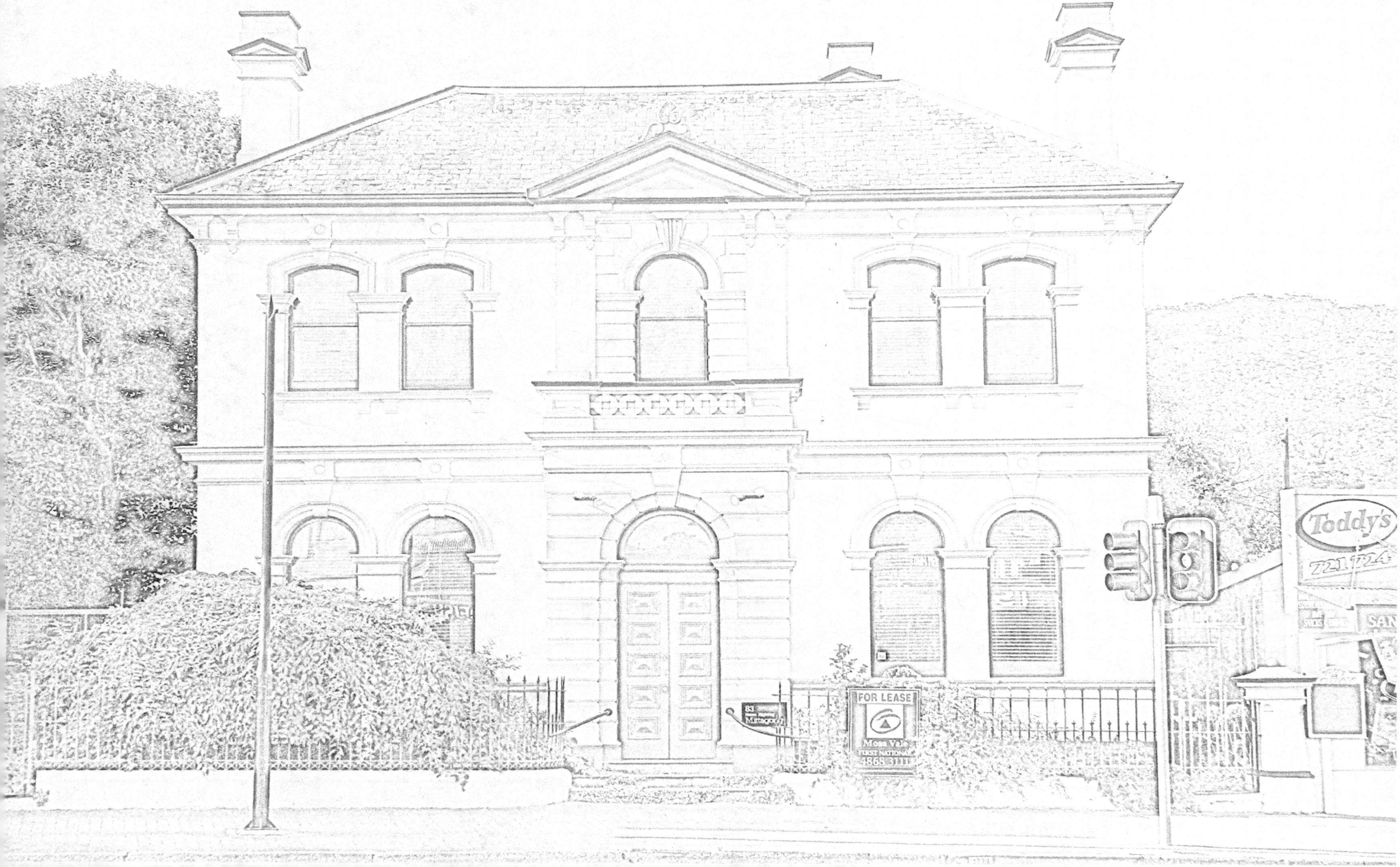
Toddy's
FOR LEASE
Moss Vale
FIRST NATIONAL

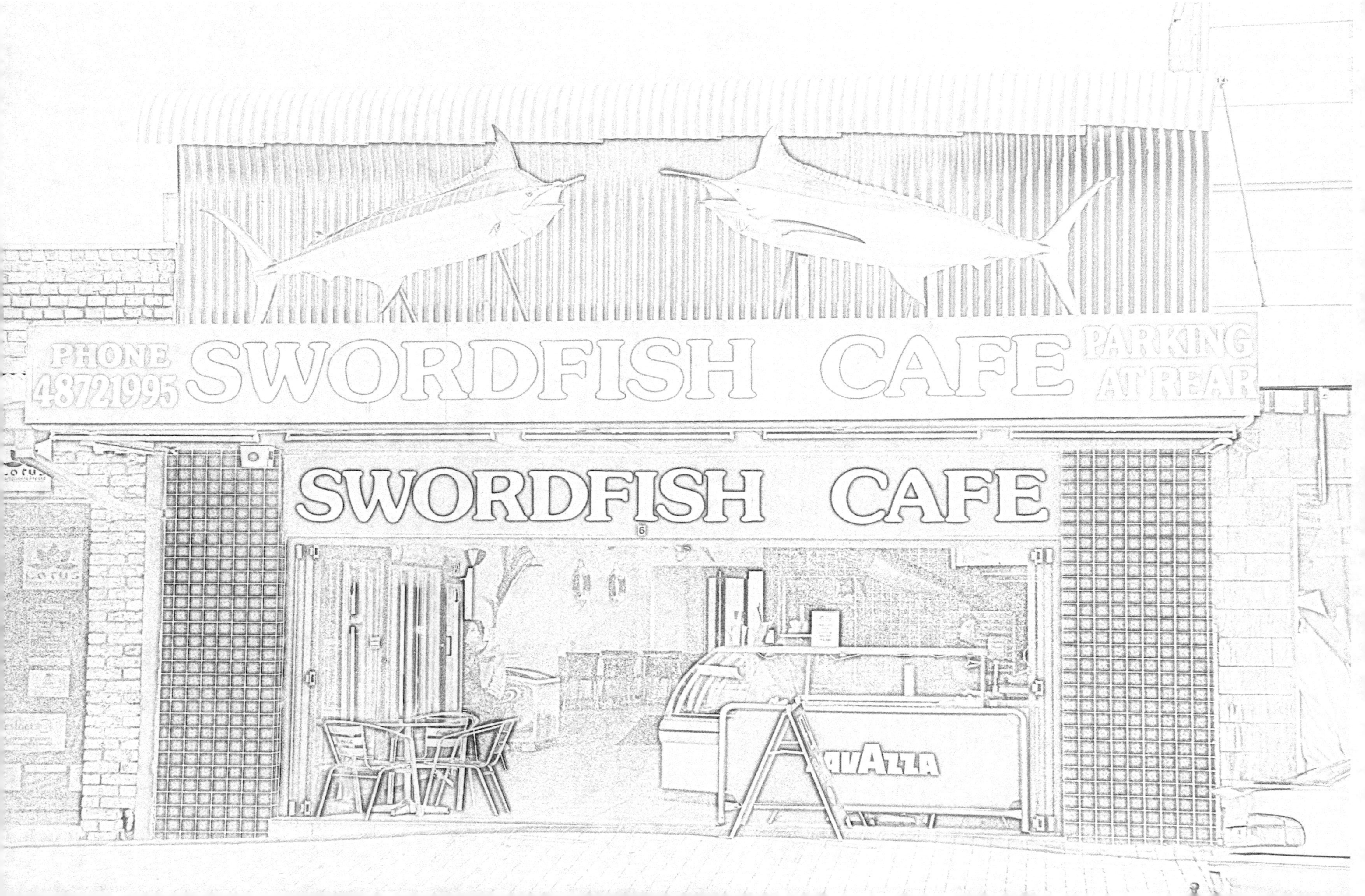
PHONE
48721995
SWORDFISH CAFE
PARKING
AT REAR
SWORDFISH CAFE
6

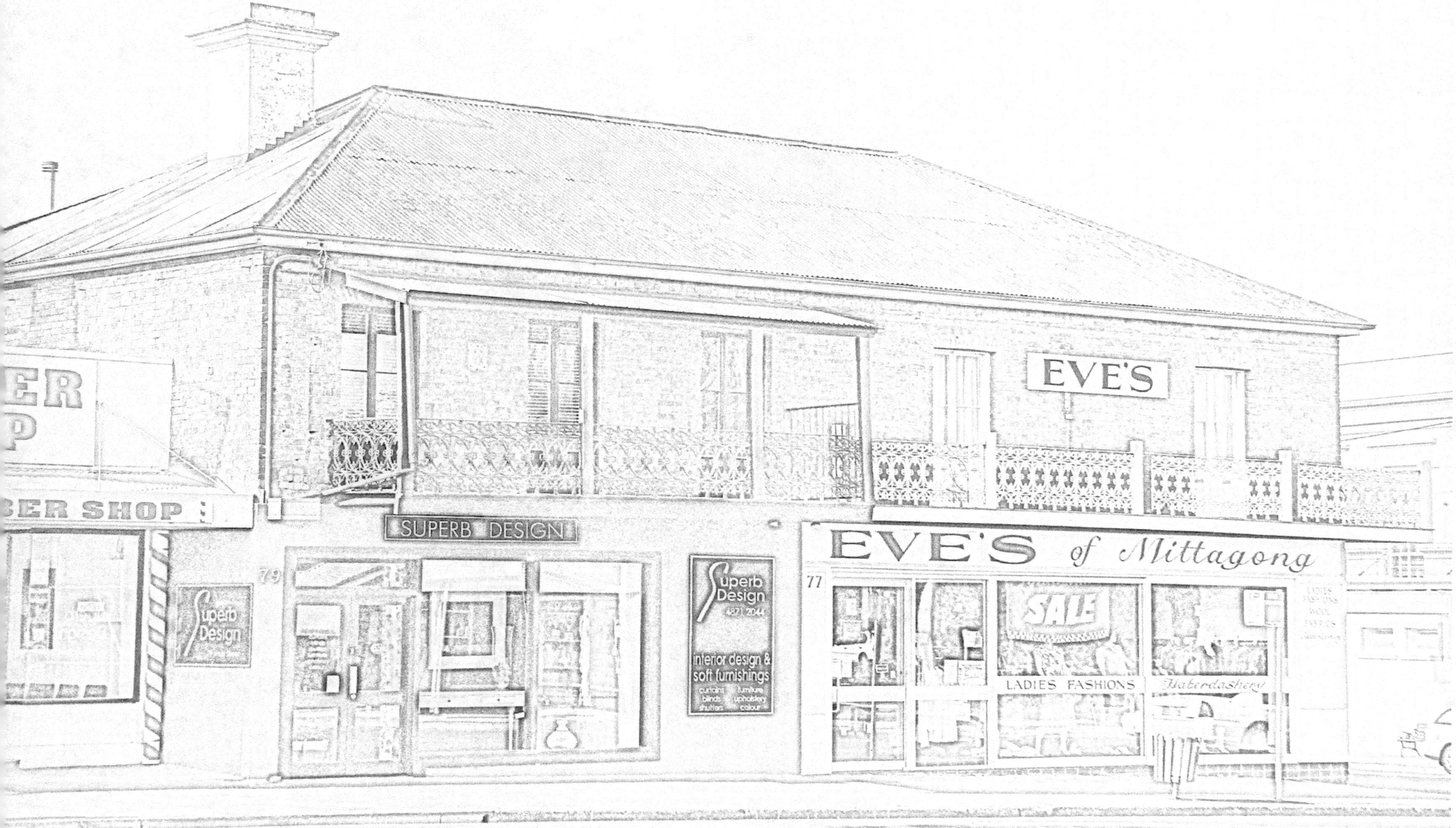
EVE'S
BER SHOP
SUPERB DESIGN
79
Superb Design
Superb Design
4871 2044
interior design &
soft furnishings
curtains
blinds
shutters
furniture
upholstery
colour
EVE'S of Mittagong
77
SALE
LADIES FASHIONS
Haberdashery

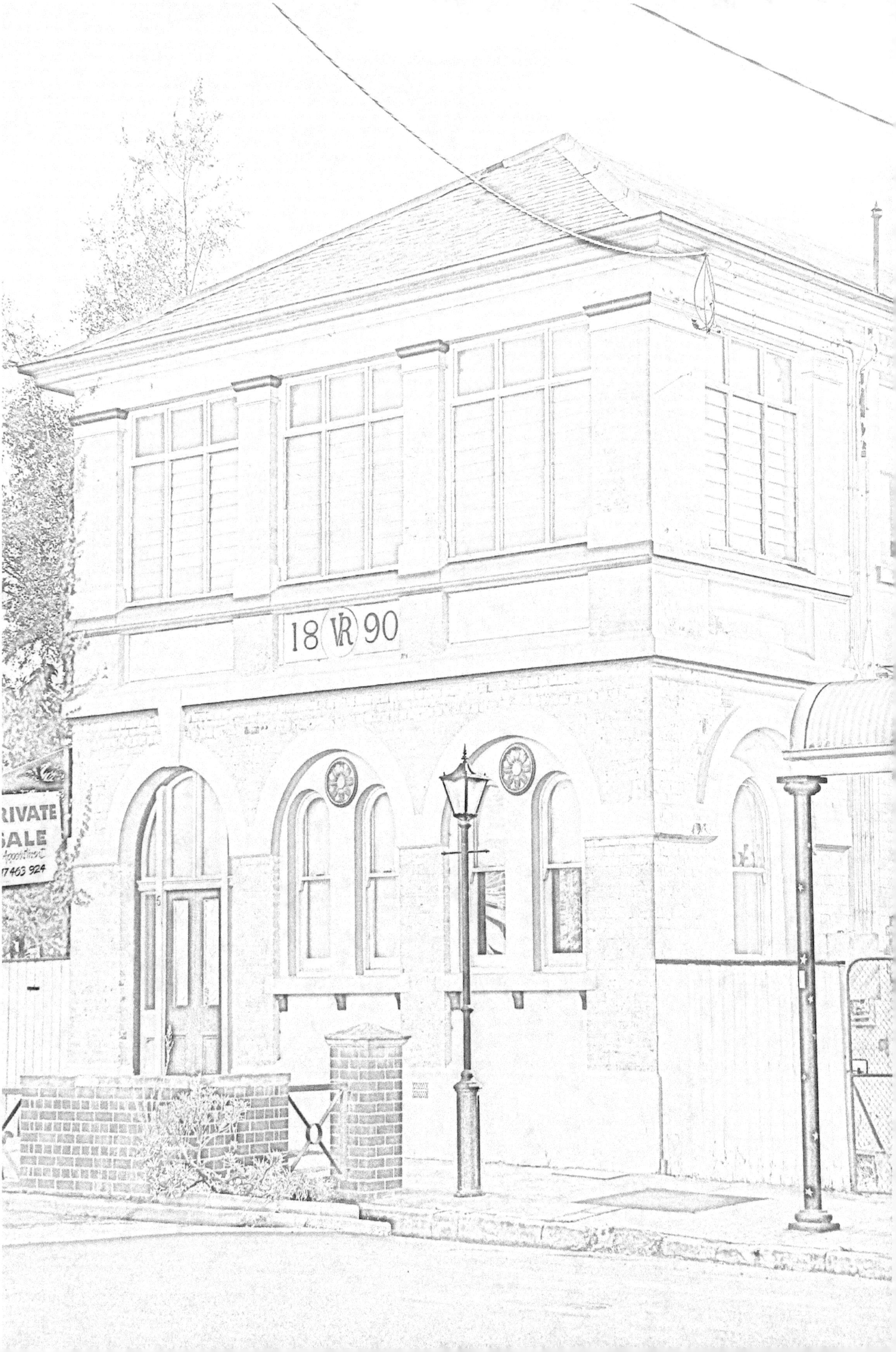
18 VR 90
RIVATE
SALE
17463 924
5

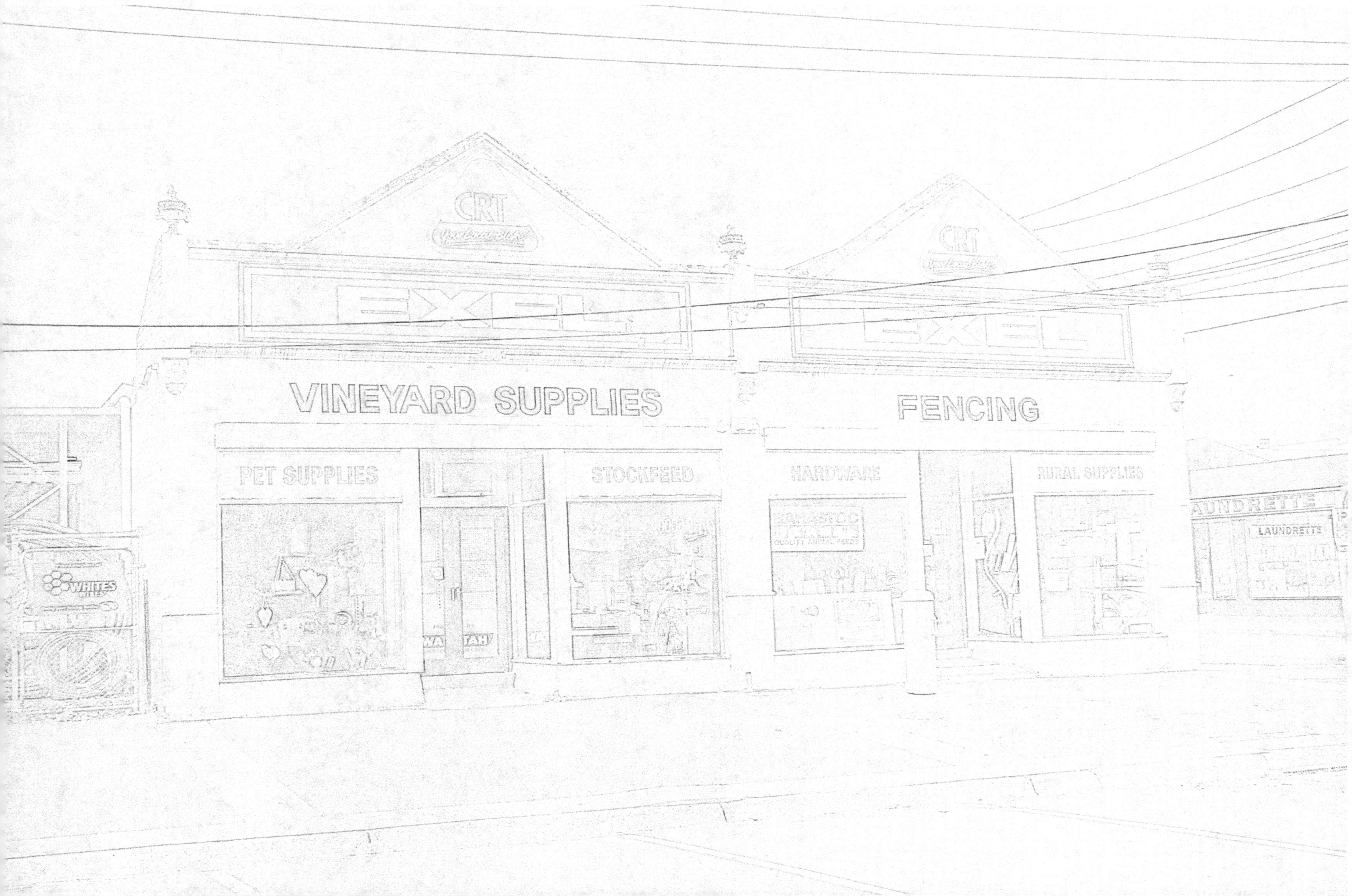
CRT
VINEYARD SUPPLIES
FENCING
PET SUPPLIES
STOCKFEED
HARDWARE
RURAL SUPPLIES
QUALITY ANIMAL FEEDS
LAUNDRETTE
LAUNDRETTE
WHITES

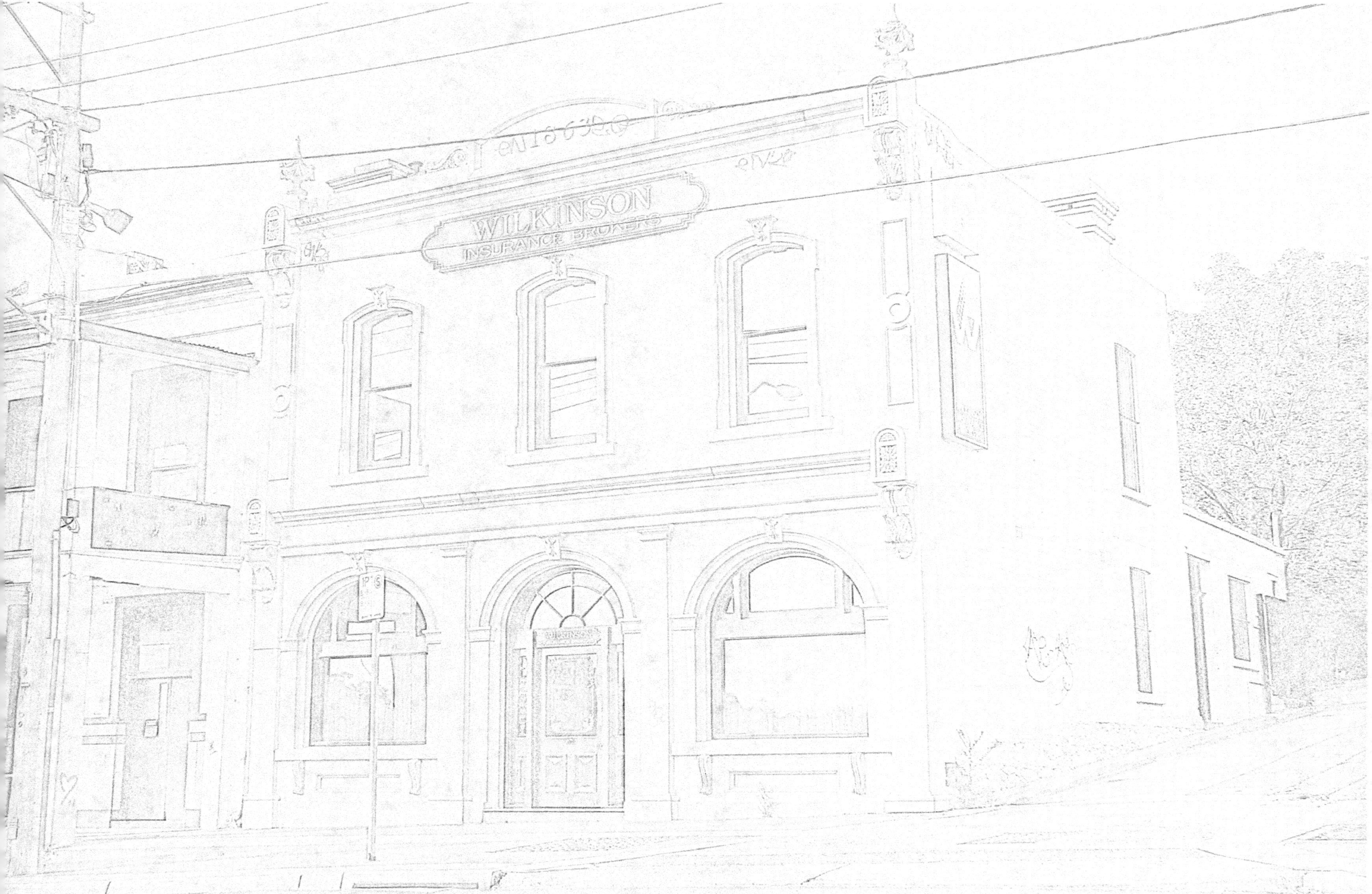
WILKINSON
INSURANCE BROKERS

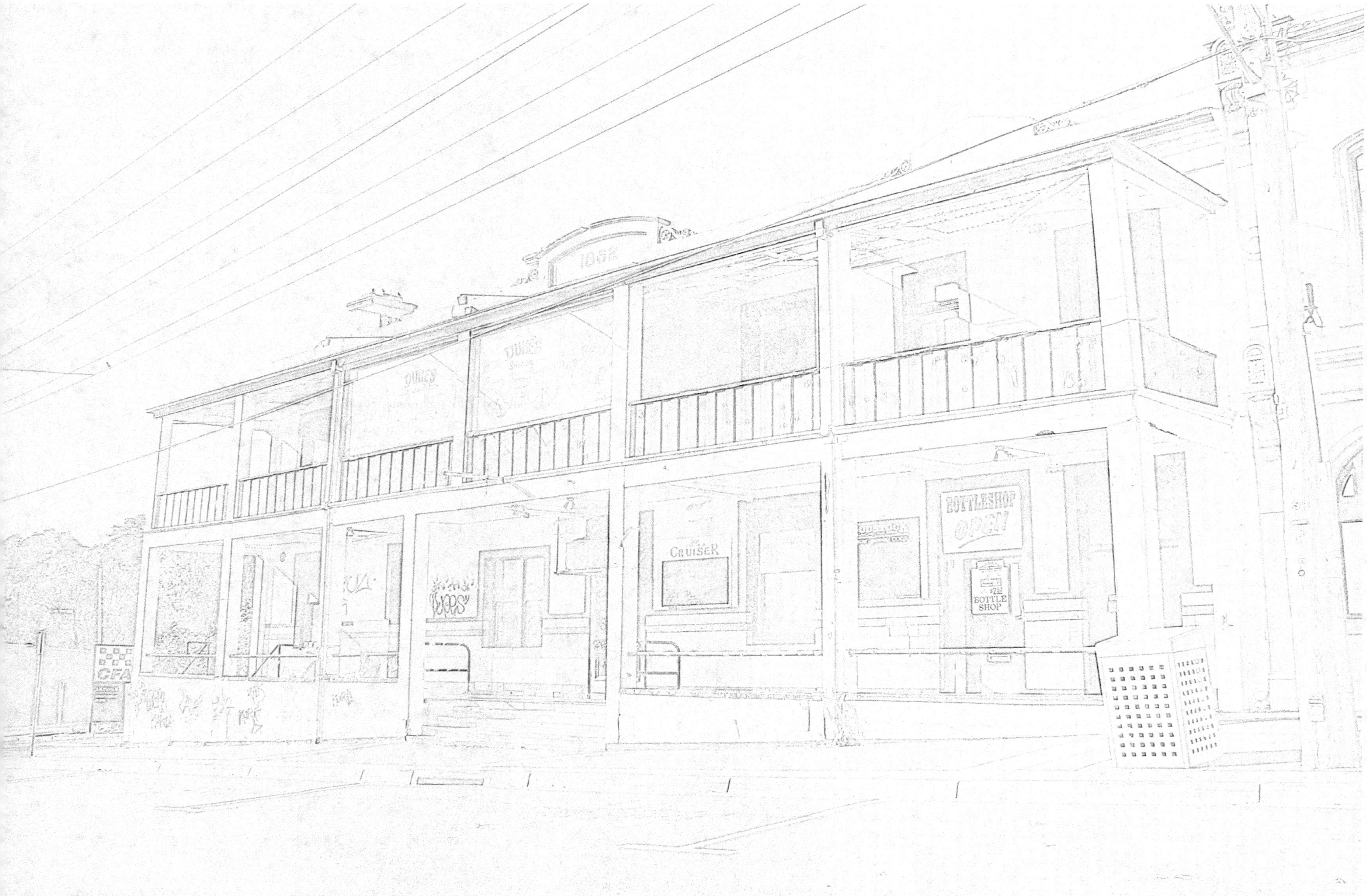
1862
CRUISER
BOTTLESHOP
OPEN
BOTTLE SHOP
CFA

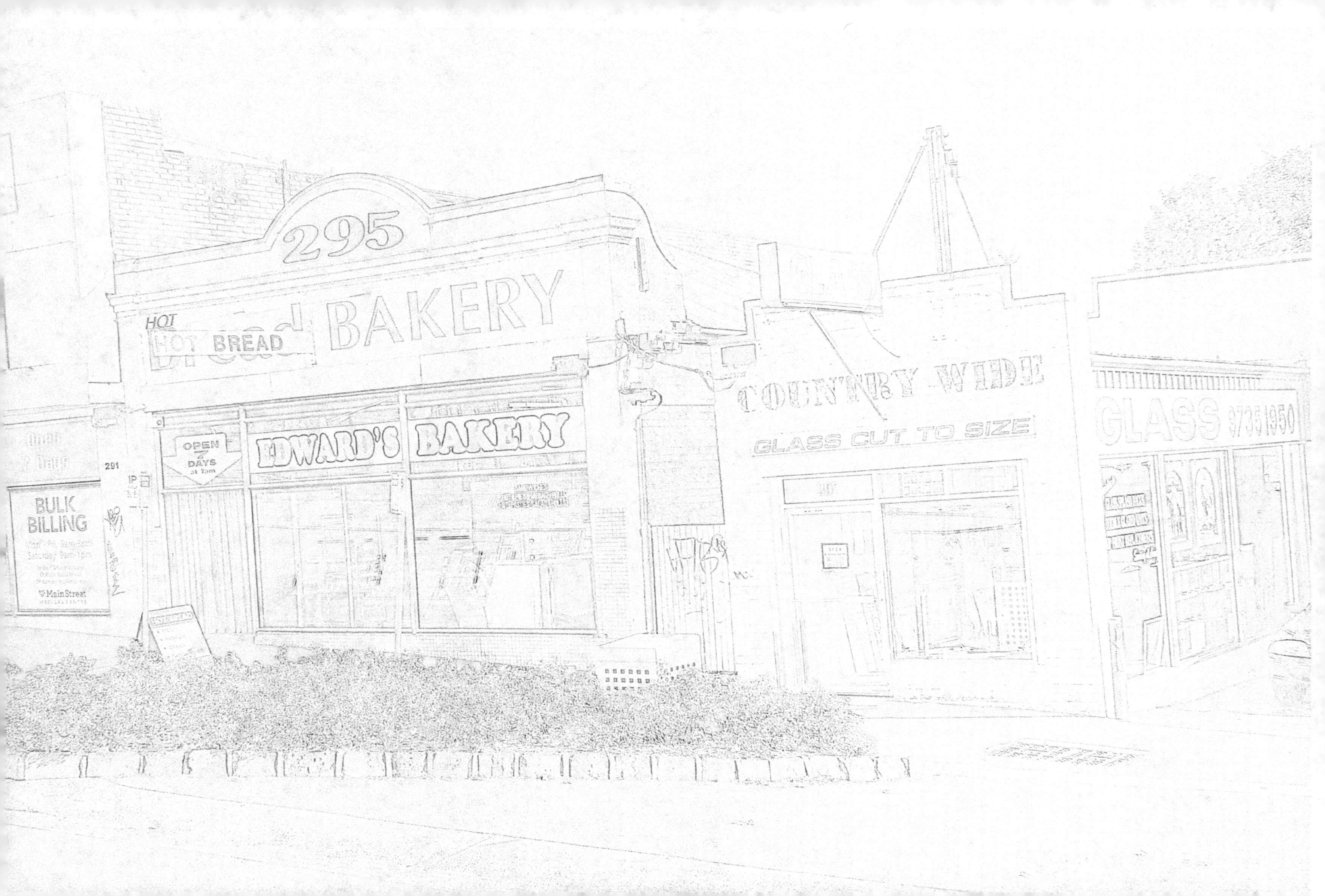
295
HOT
HOT BREAD
BAKERY
OPEN 7 DAYS at 7am
EDWARD'S BAKERY
BULK BILLING
Main Street
291
COUNTRY WIDE
GLASS CUT TO SIZE
GLASS 9735 1950

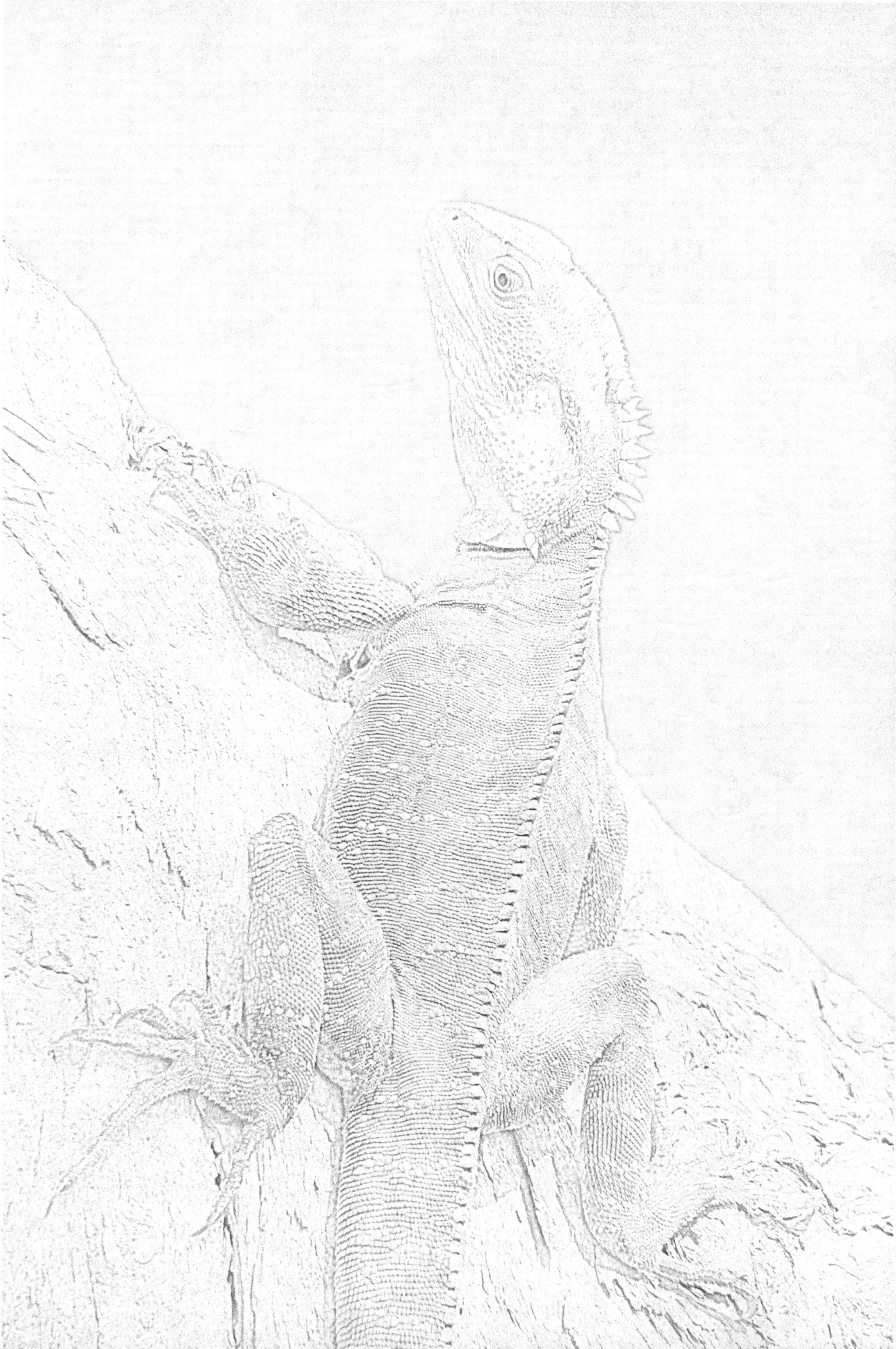

PARSONS
HISTORIC STORE
OLDE WORLD GIFTS
SV
3M

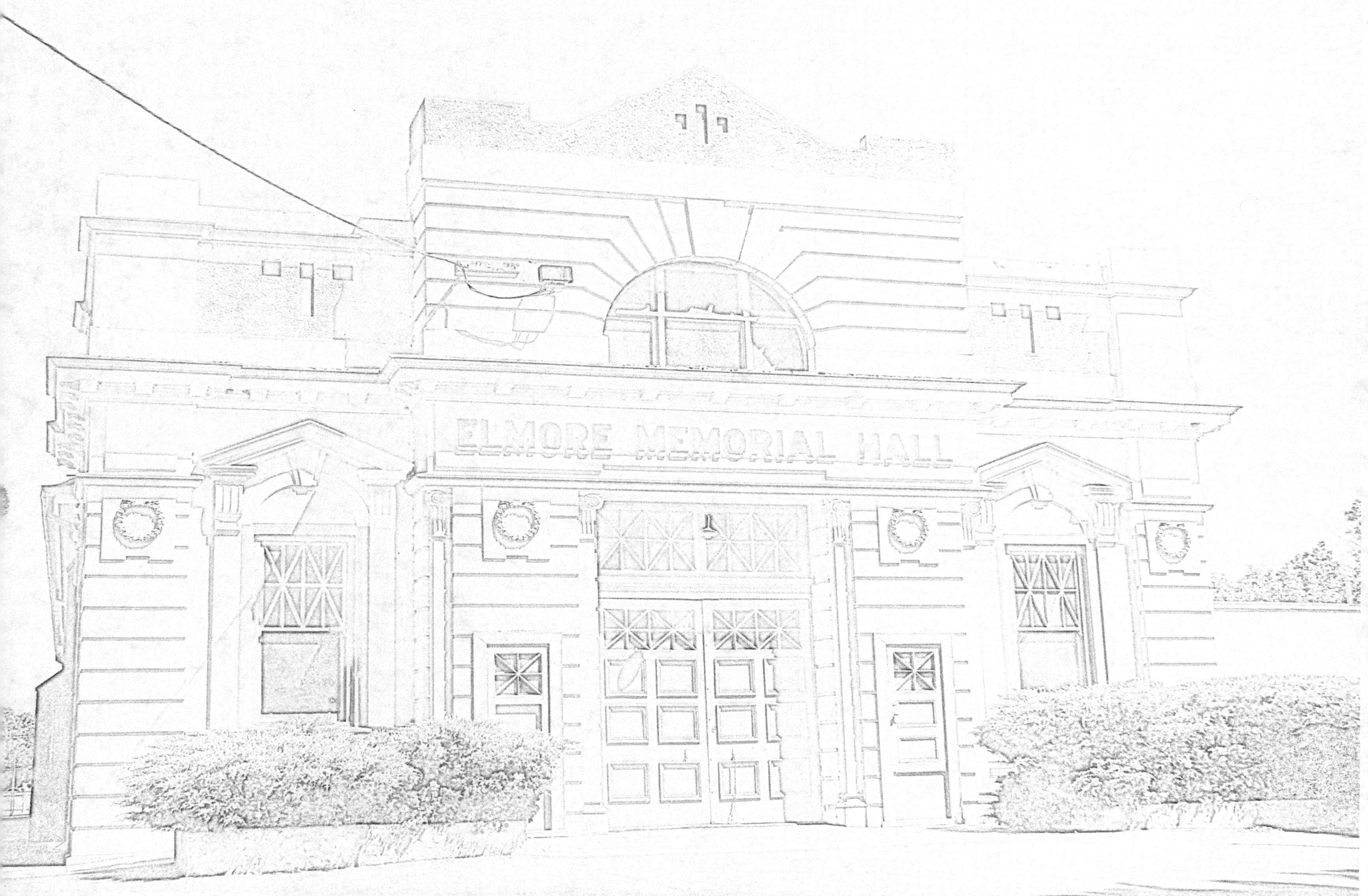
ELMORE MEMORIAL HALL

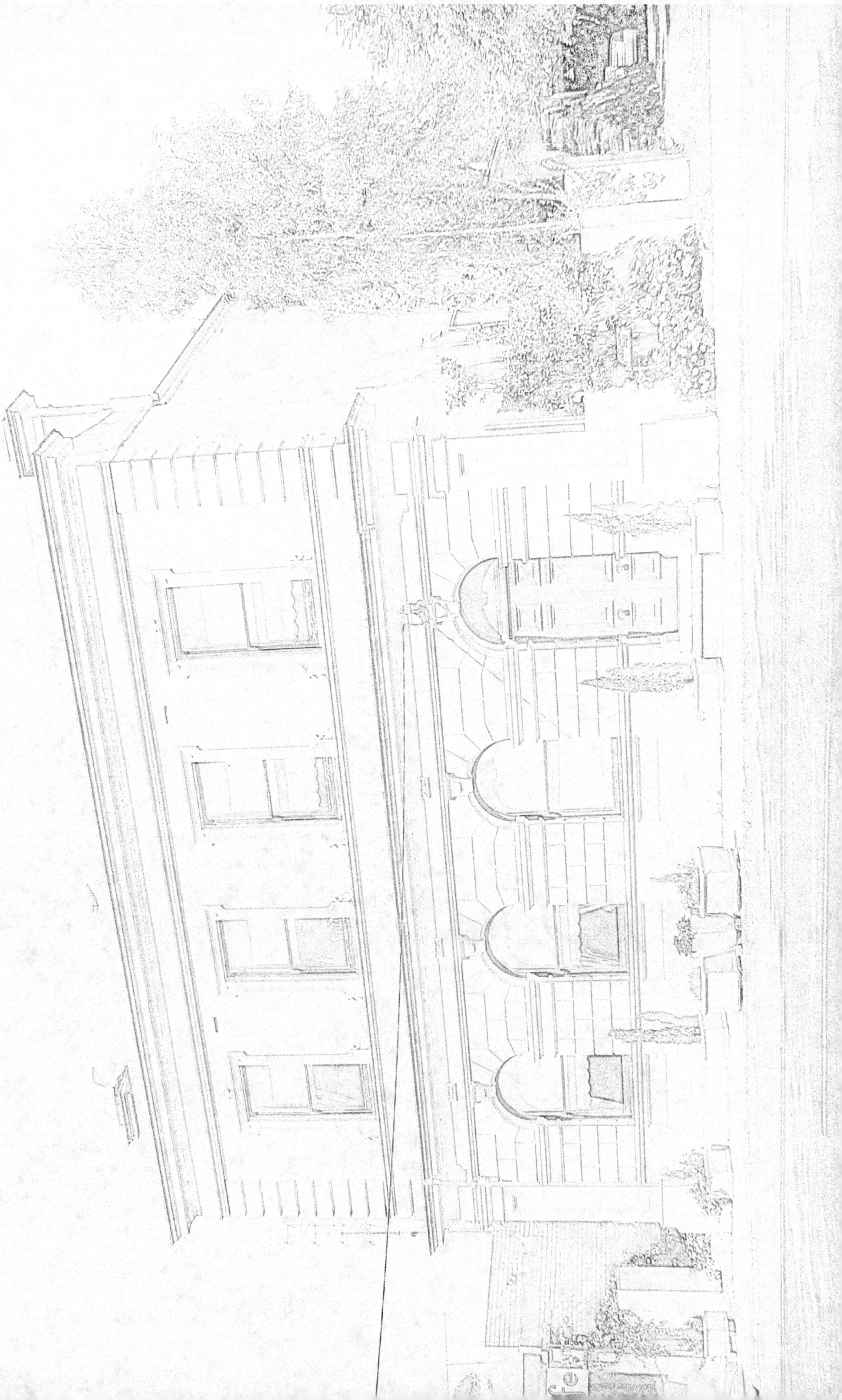

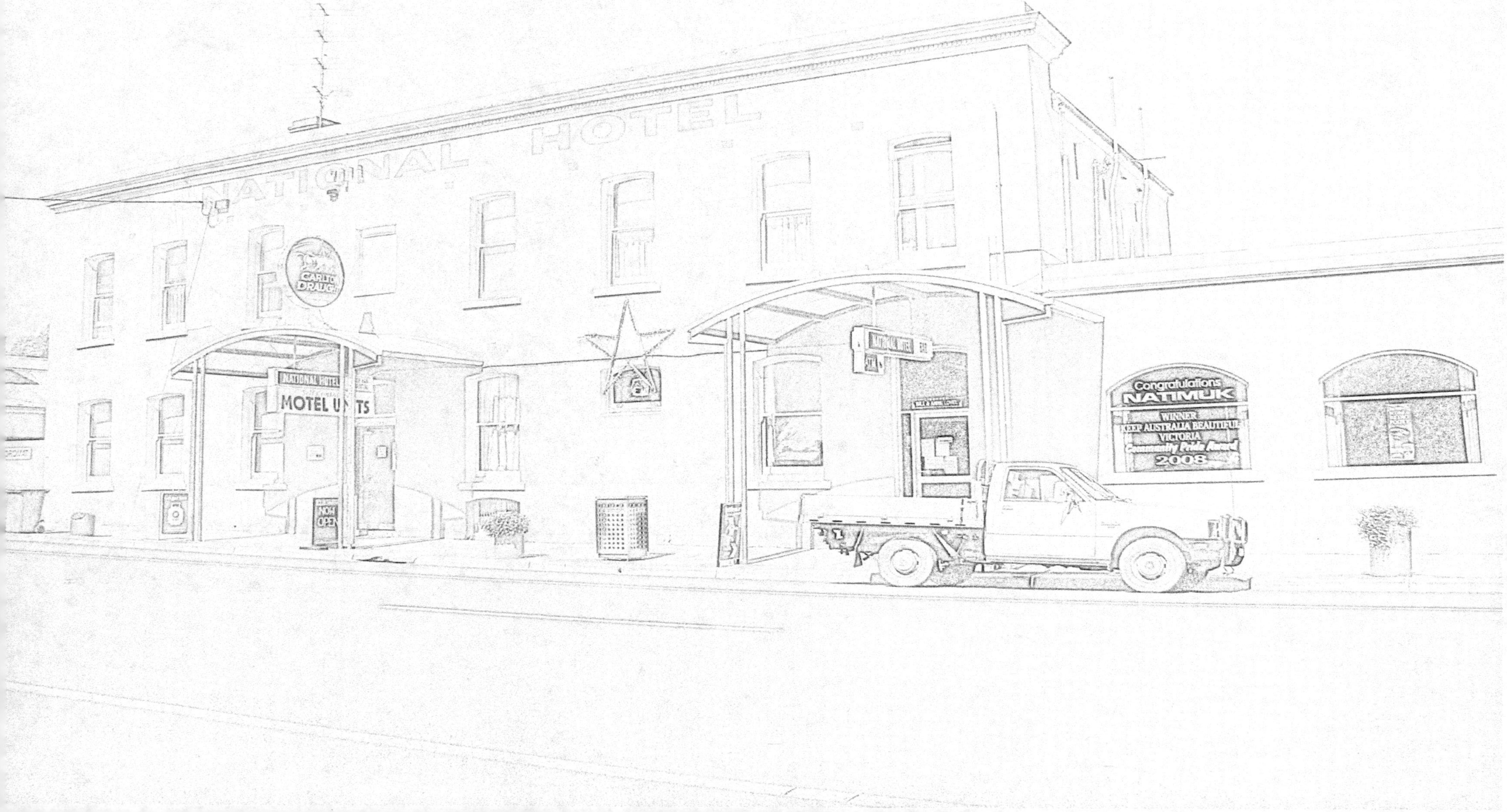
NATIONAL HOTEL
CARLTON DRAUGHT
NATIONAL HOTEL
MOTEL UNITS
NOW OPEN
Congratulations
NATIMUK
WINNER
KEEP AUSTRALIA BEAUTIFUL
VICTORIA
Community Pride Award
2008

COURT HOUSE

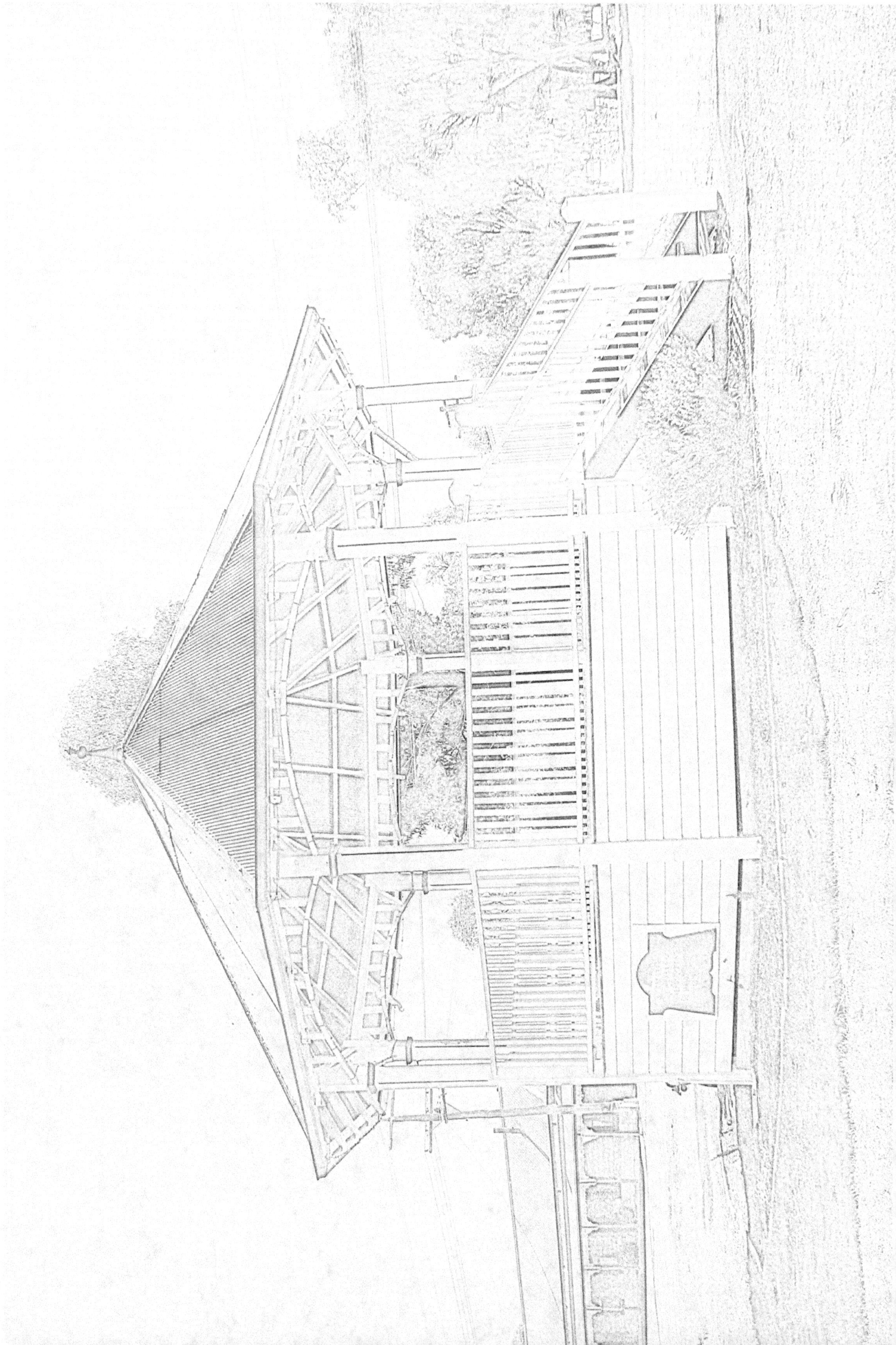

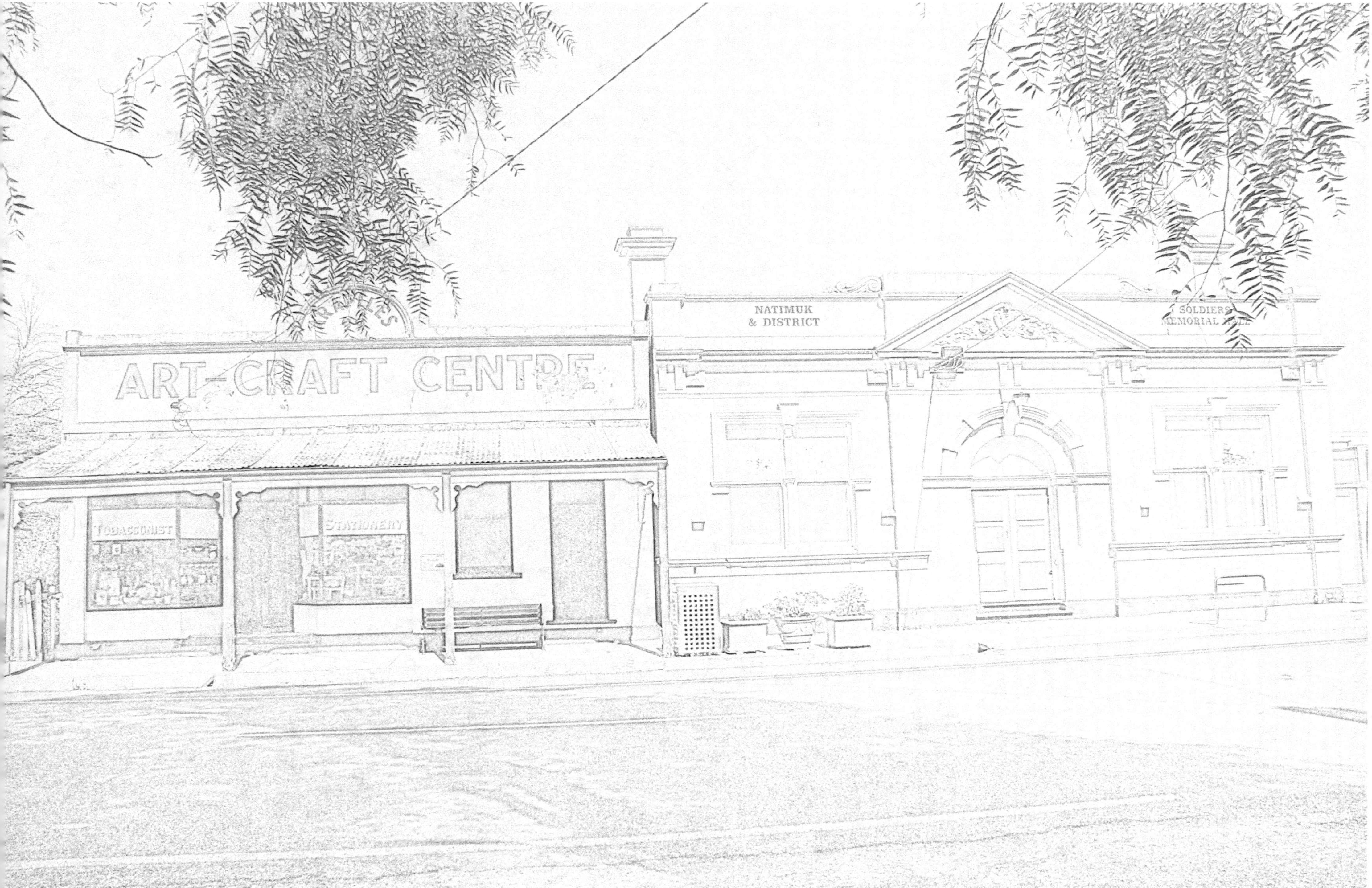
ART-CRAFT CENTRE
TOBACCONIST
STATIONERY
NATIMUK
& DISTRICT
SOLDIERS
MEMORIAL HALL

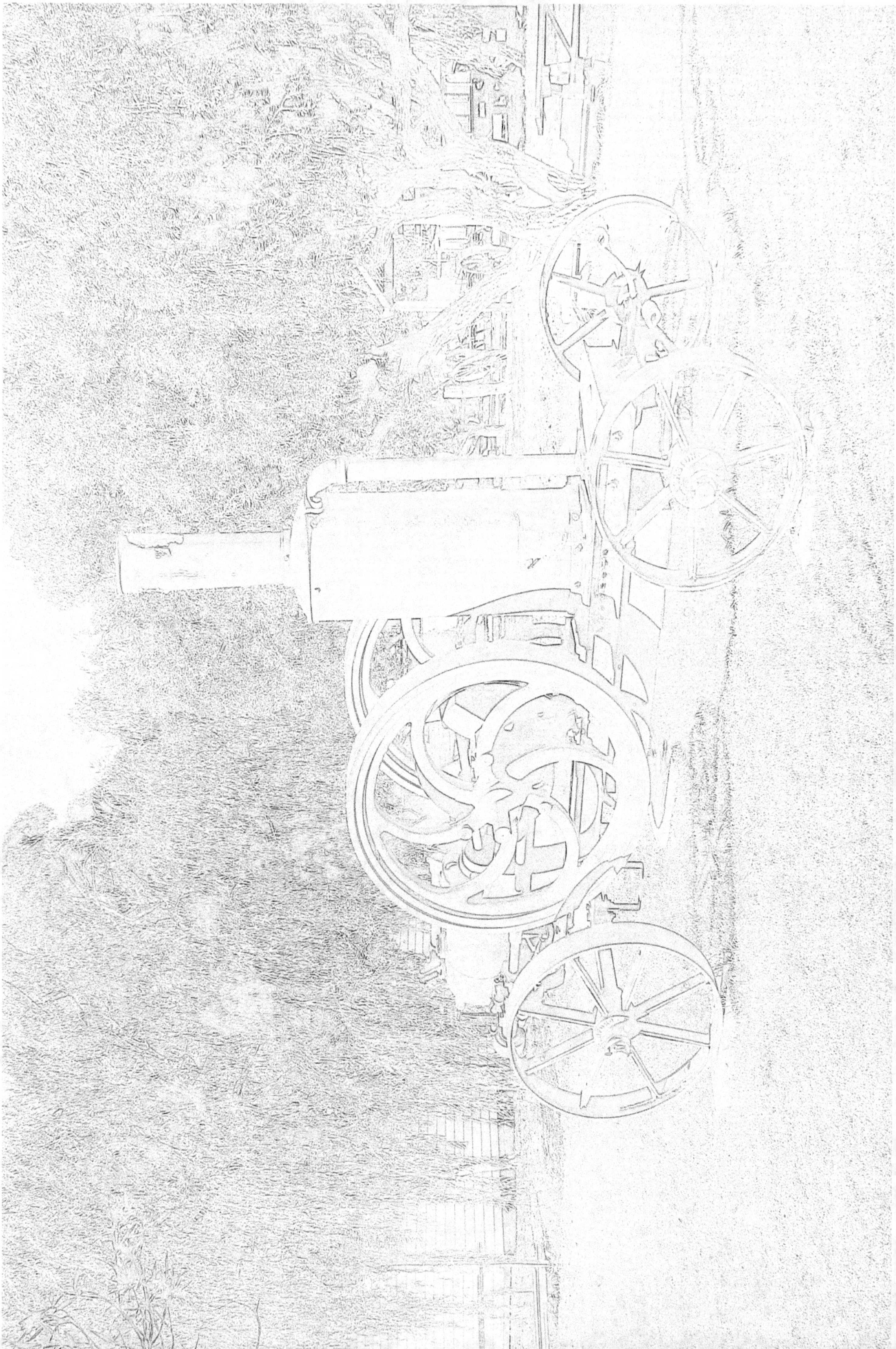

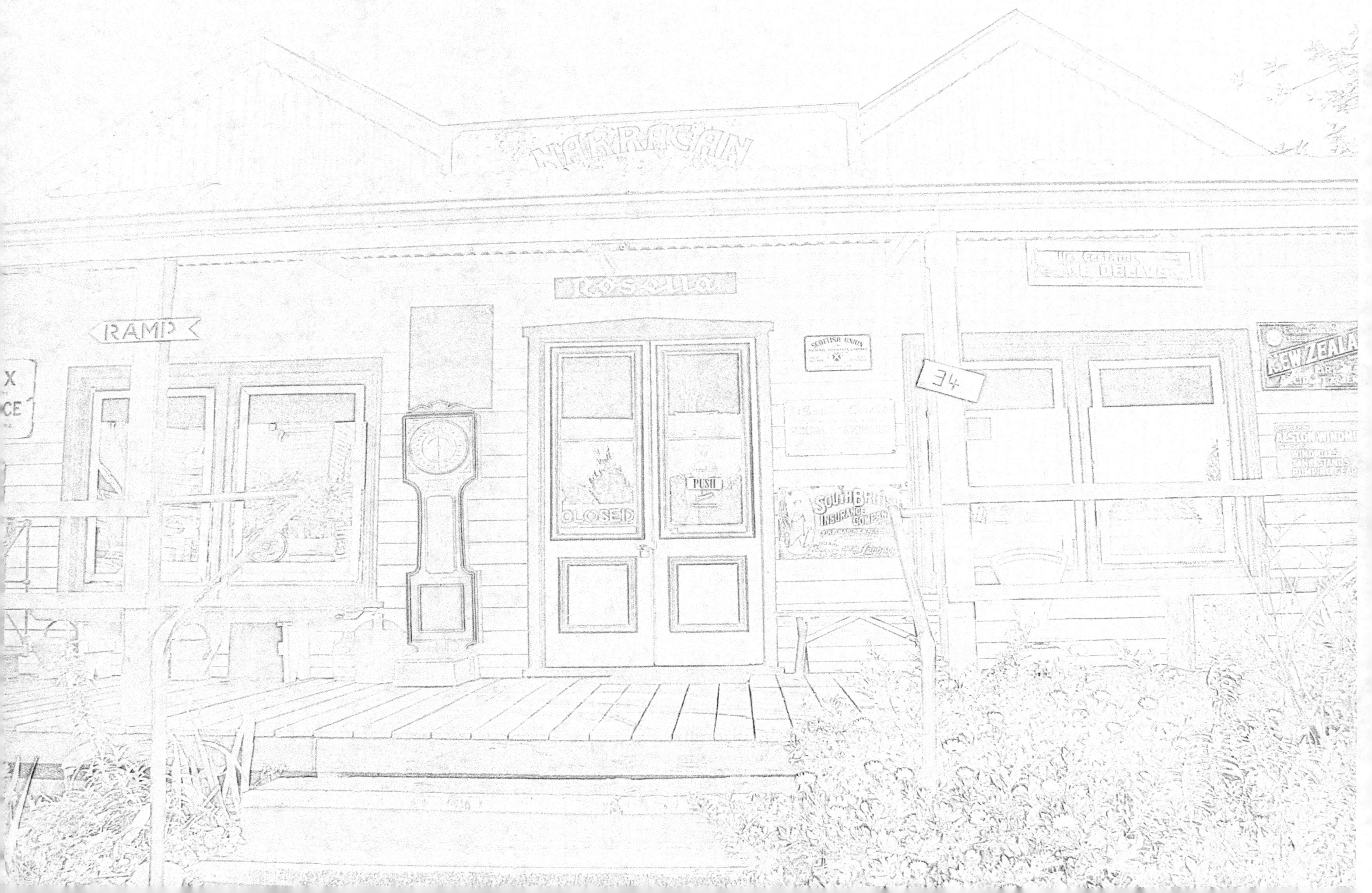
NARRACAN
RAMP
SCOTTISH UNION
34
CLOSED
PUSH
SOUTH BRIT
INSURANCE COMPAN
NEW ZEALA
ALSTON WINDMI

THE NATIONAL BANK OF AUSTRALASIA LTD.
NATIONAL BANK
NATIONAL BANK
GAOL

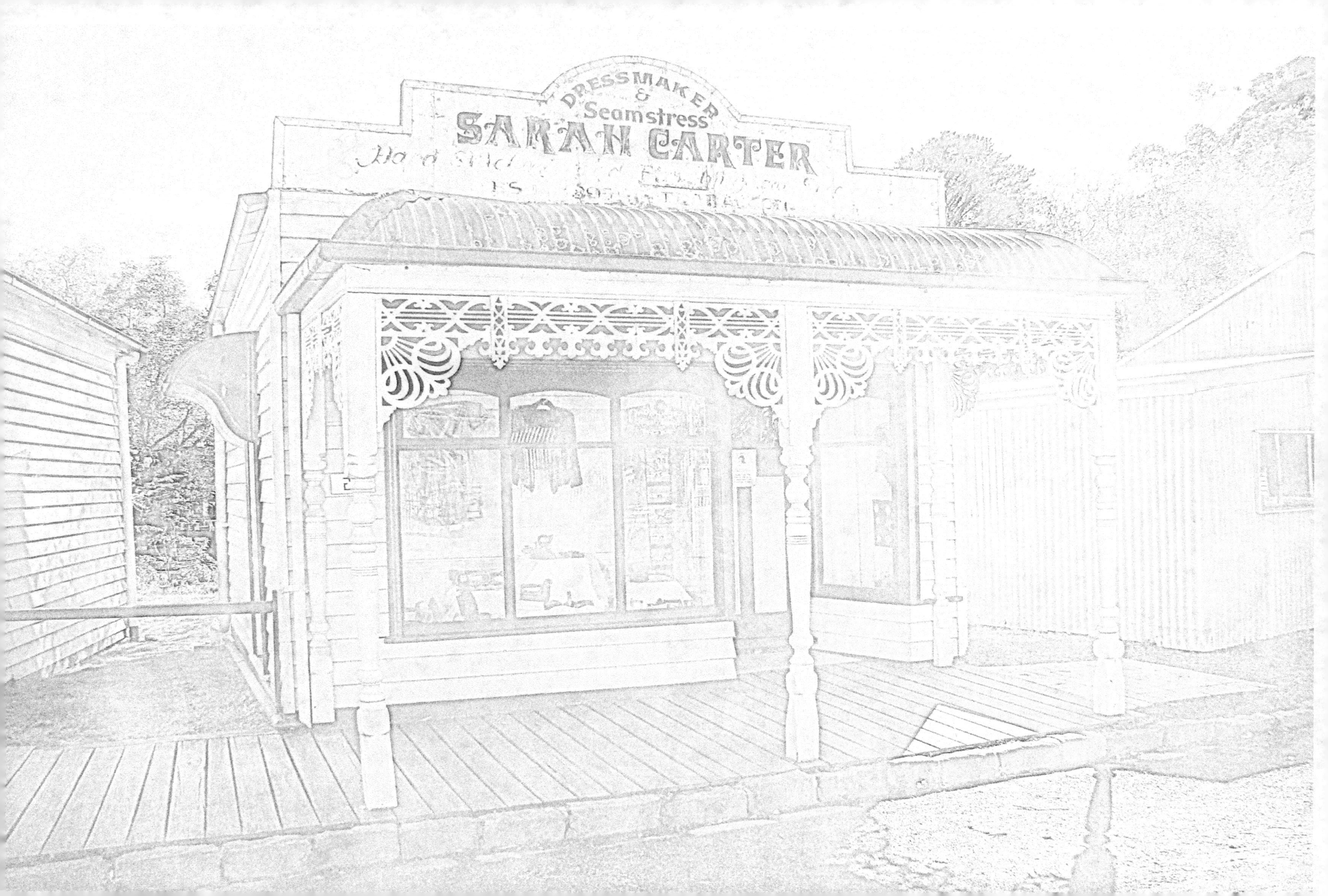
DRESSMAKER
&
Seamstress
SARAH CARTER

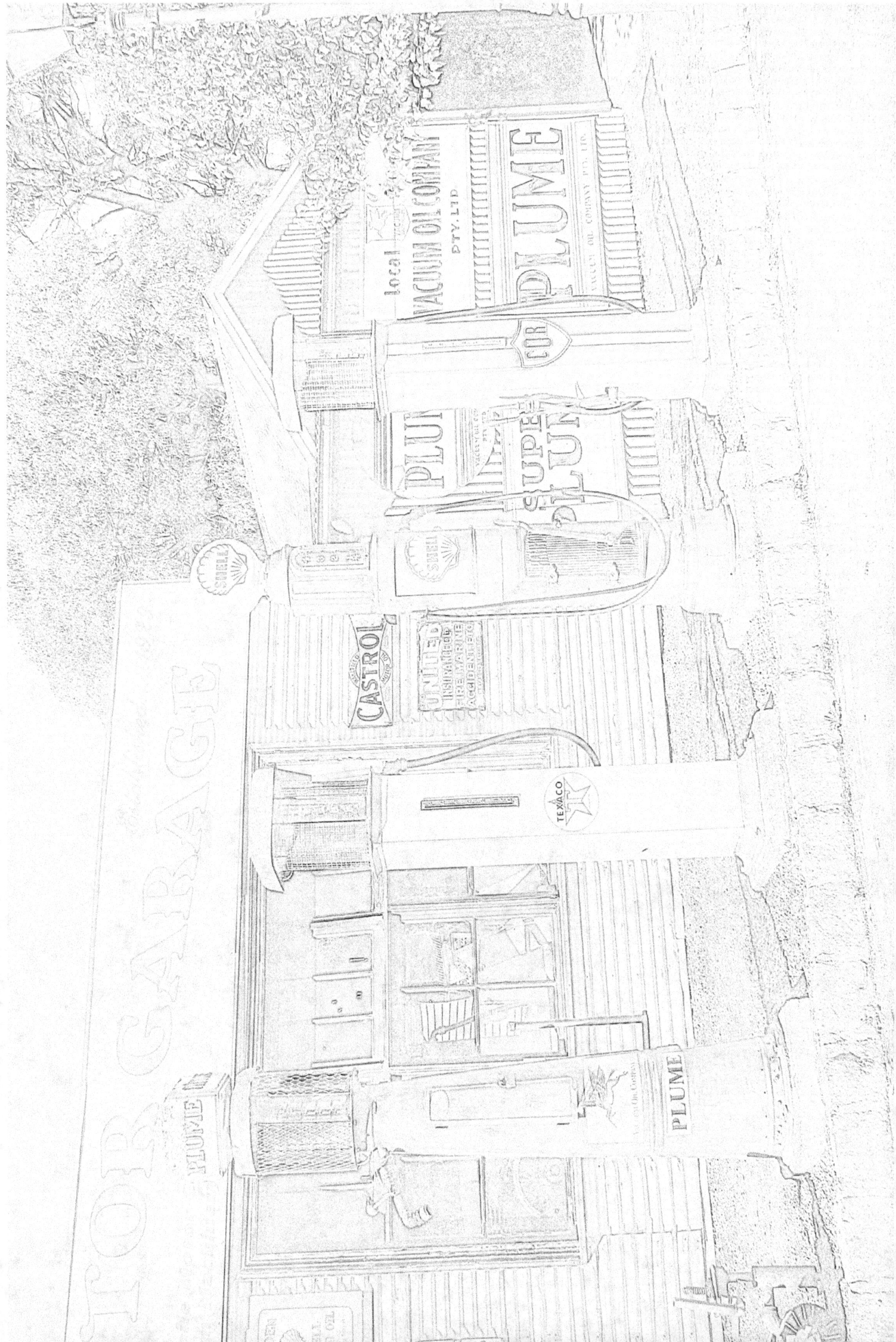
GARAGE
Local
VACUUM OIL COMPANY
PTY. LTD
PLUME
SHELL
CASTROL
UNITED
TEXACO
PLUME
PLUME

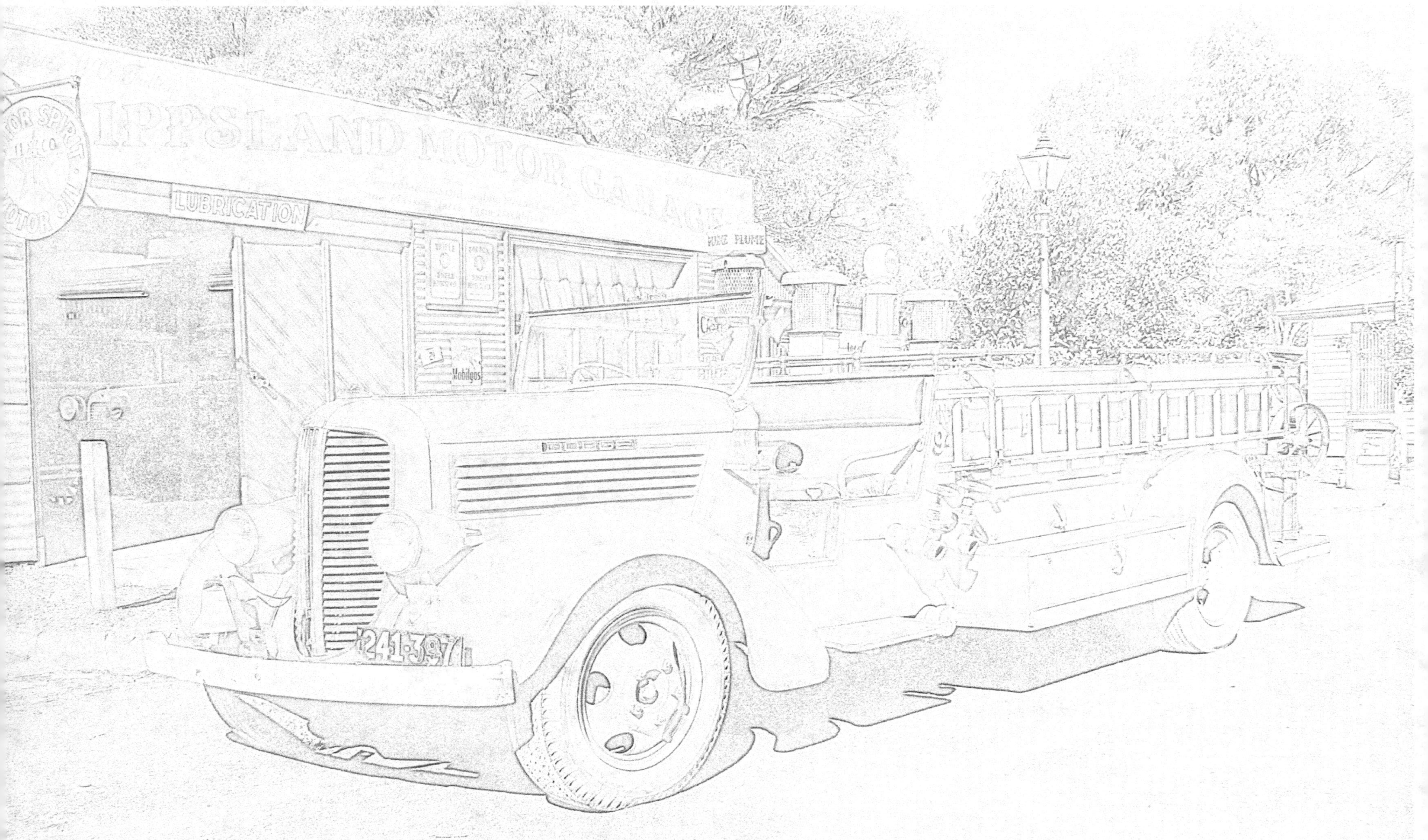
IPPSLAND MOTOR GARAGE
LUBRICATION
PURE FLUME
Mobilgas
241-397

COBB & CO
COBB & Cº INN
19
BITTER
ALE

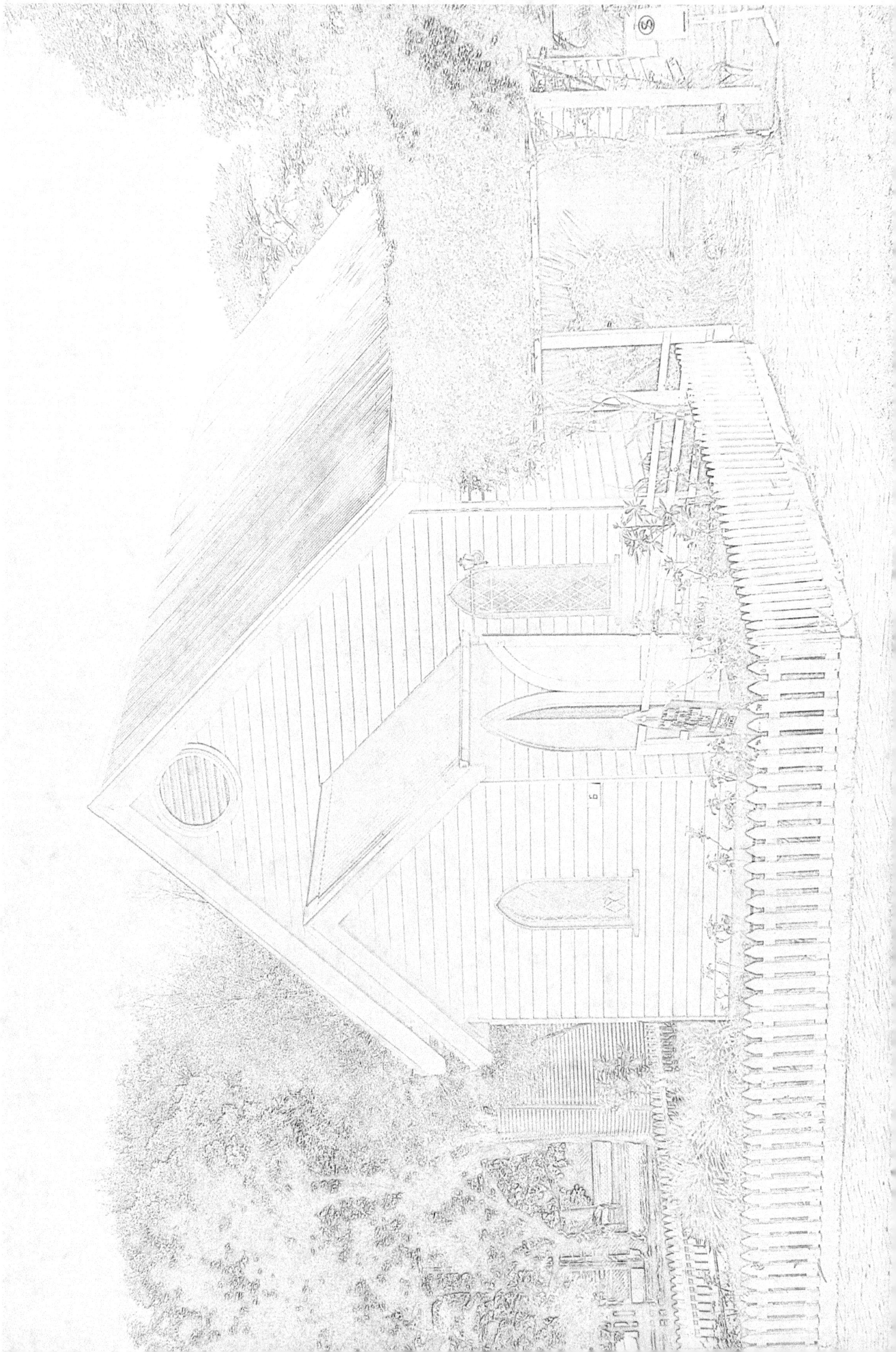

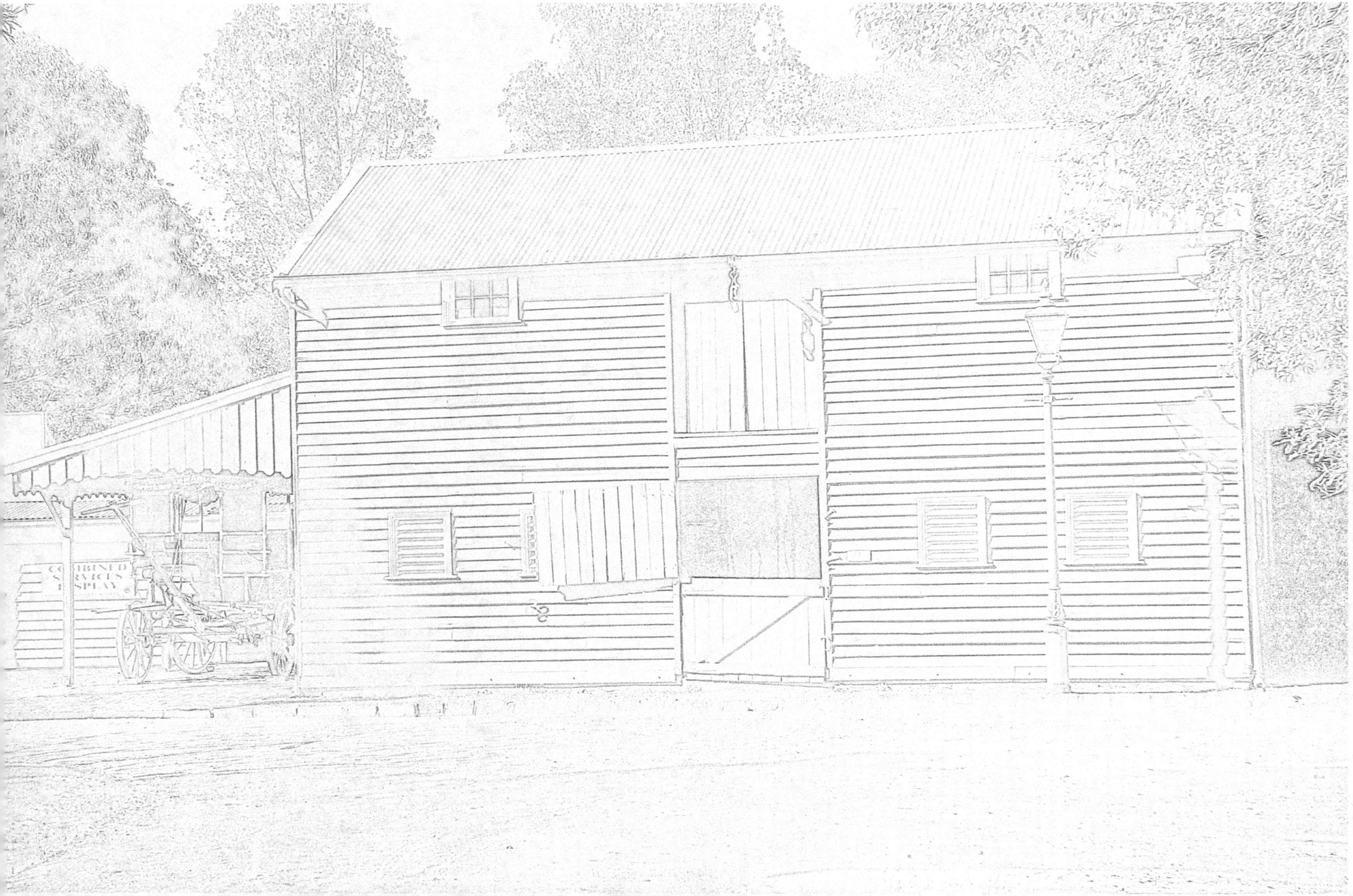

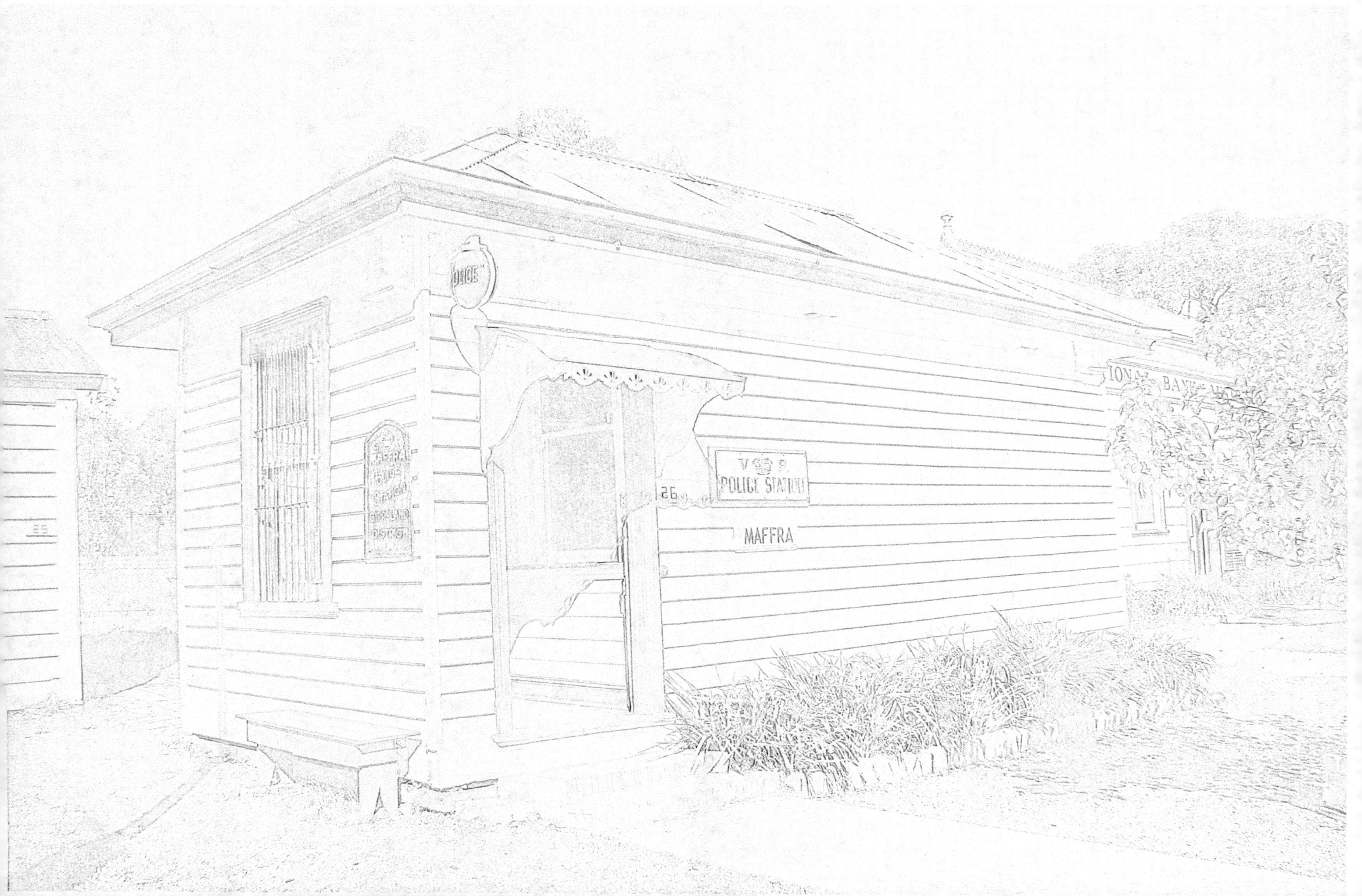
POLICE
V R
POLICE STATION
MAFFRA
26
25

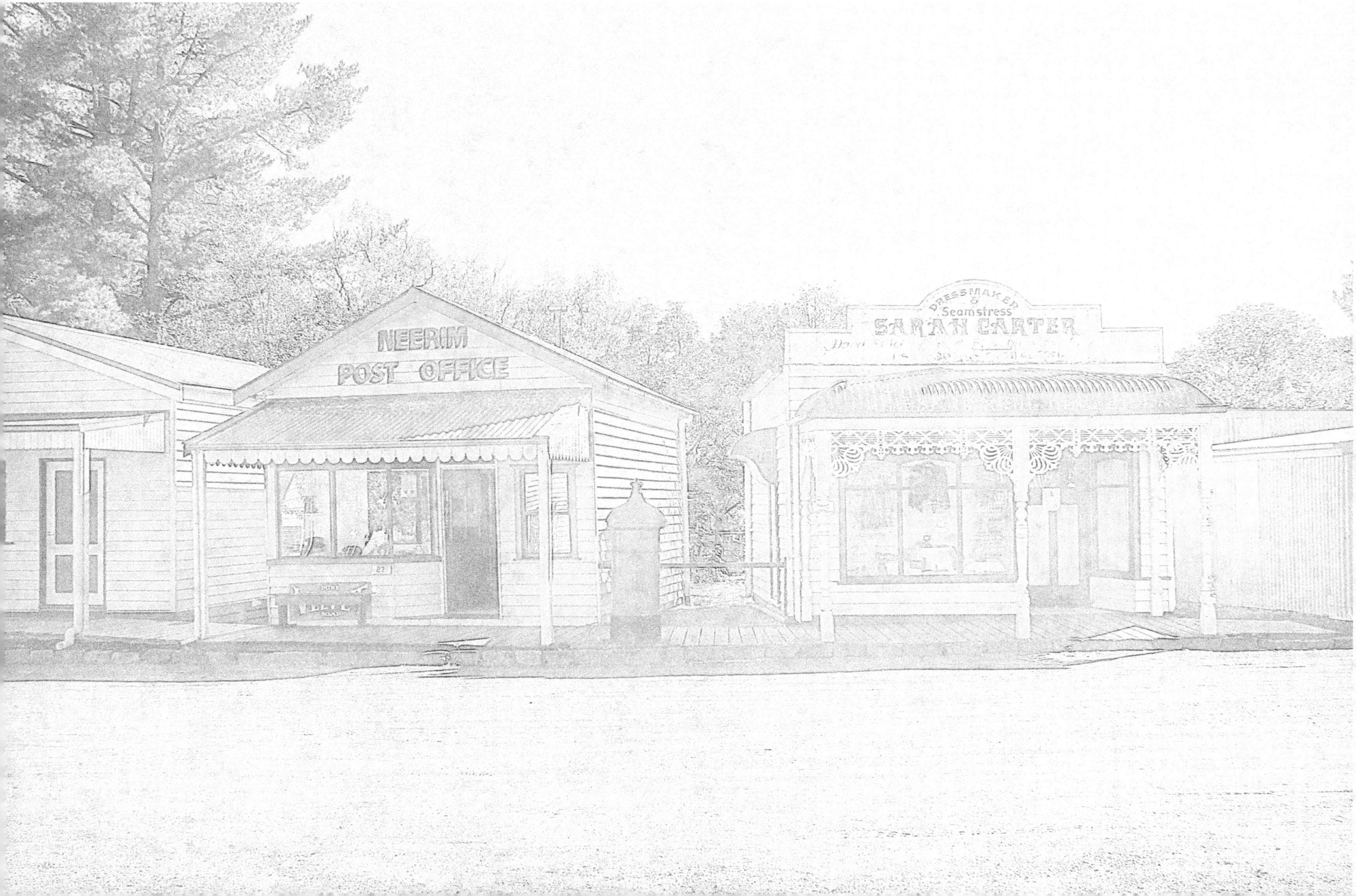
NEERIM
POST OFFICE
27
DRESSMAKER
&
Seamstress
SARAH CARTER

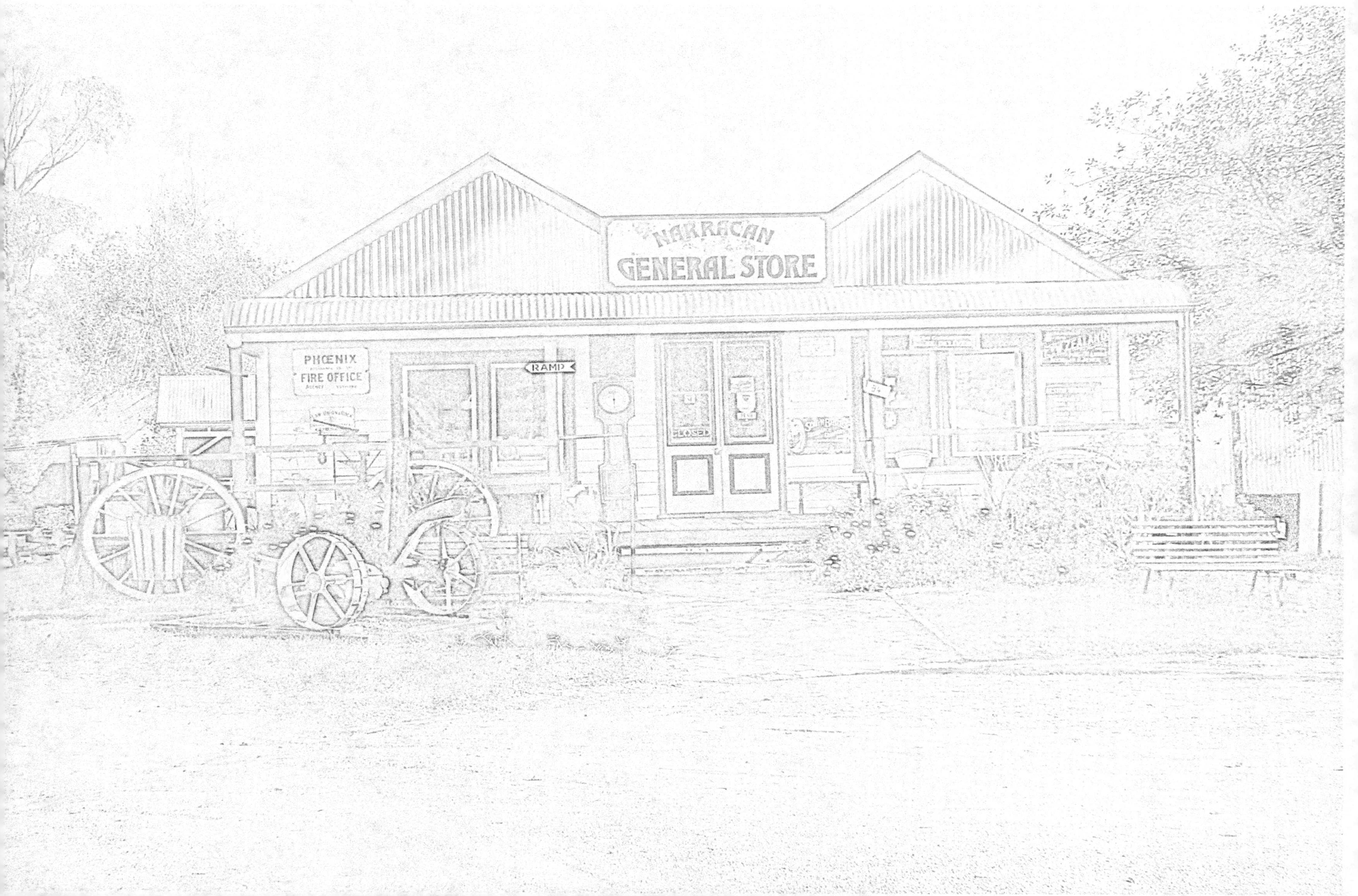
NARRACAN
GENERAL STORE
PHŒNIX
FIRE OFFICE
RAMP
CLOSED

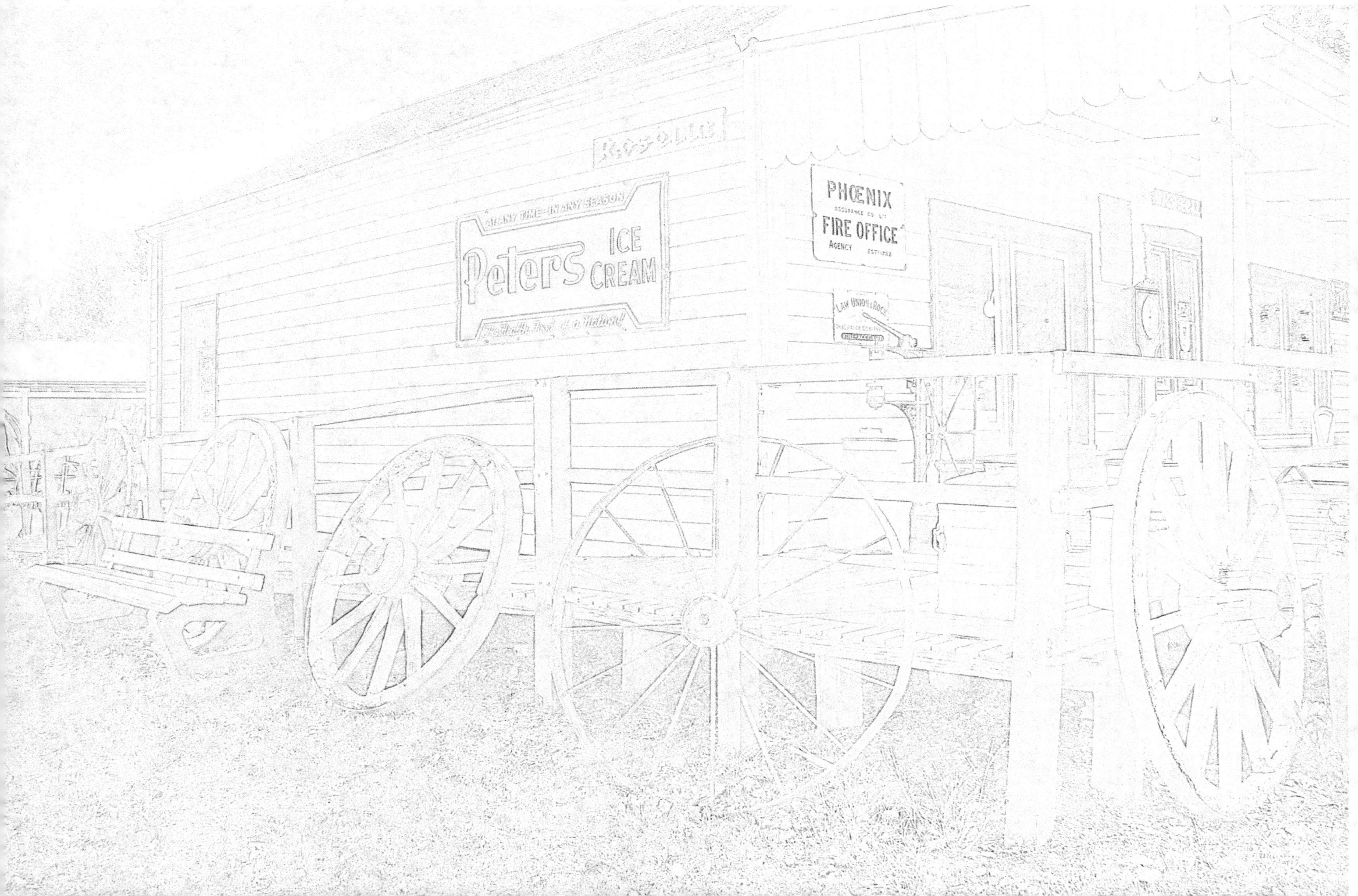
AT ANY TIME—IN ANY SEASON
Peters ICE CREAM
PHŒNIX
ASSURANCE CO. LTD
FIRE OFFICE
AGENCY EST 1782
LAW UNION & ROCK

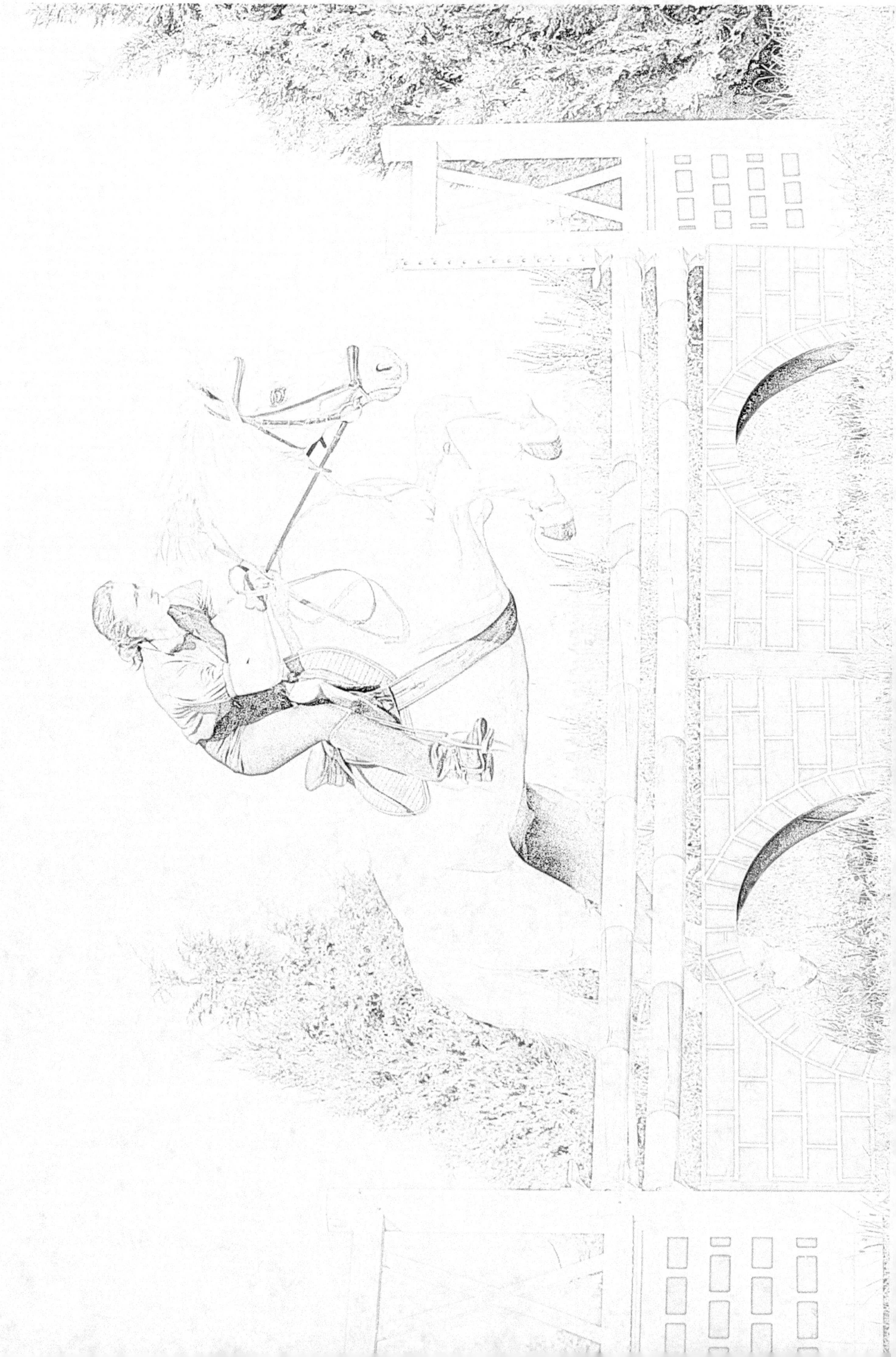

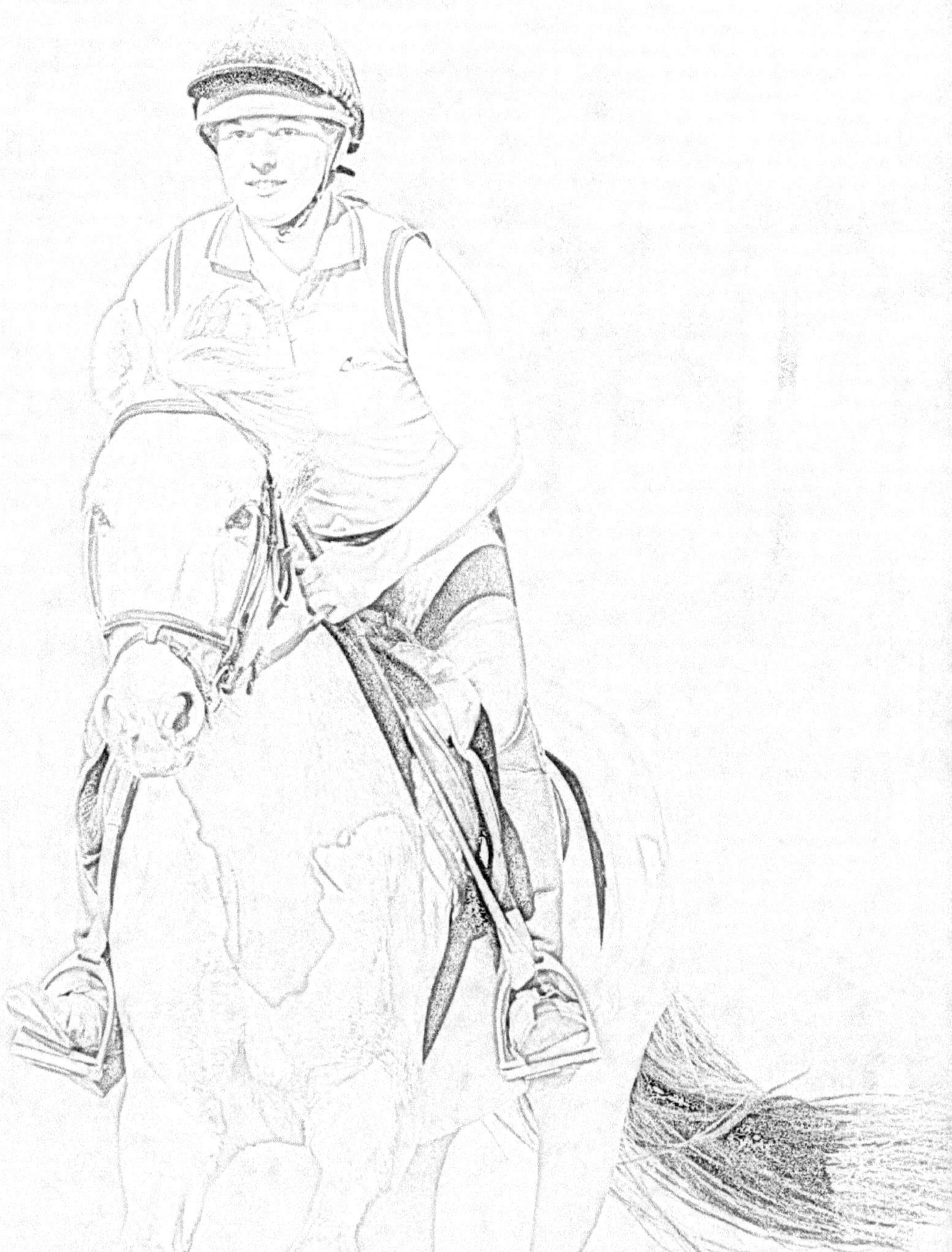

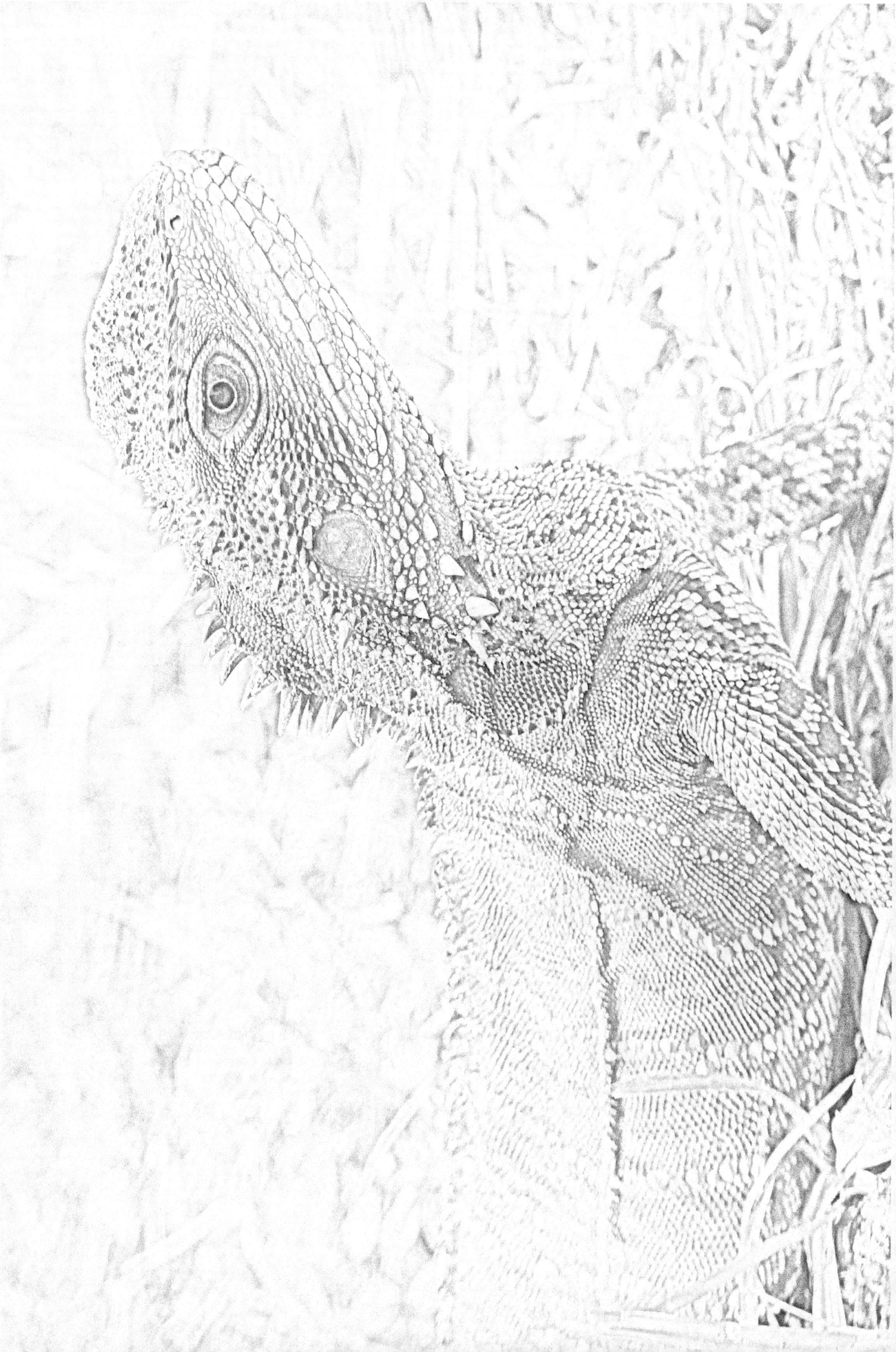

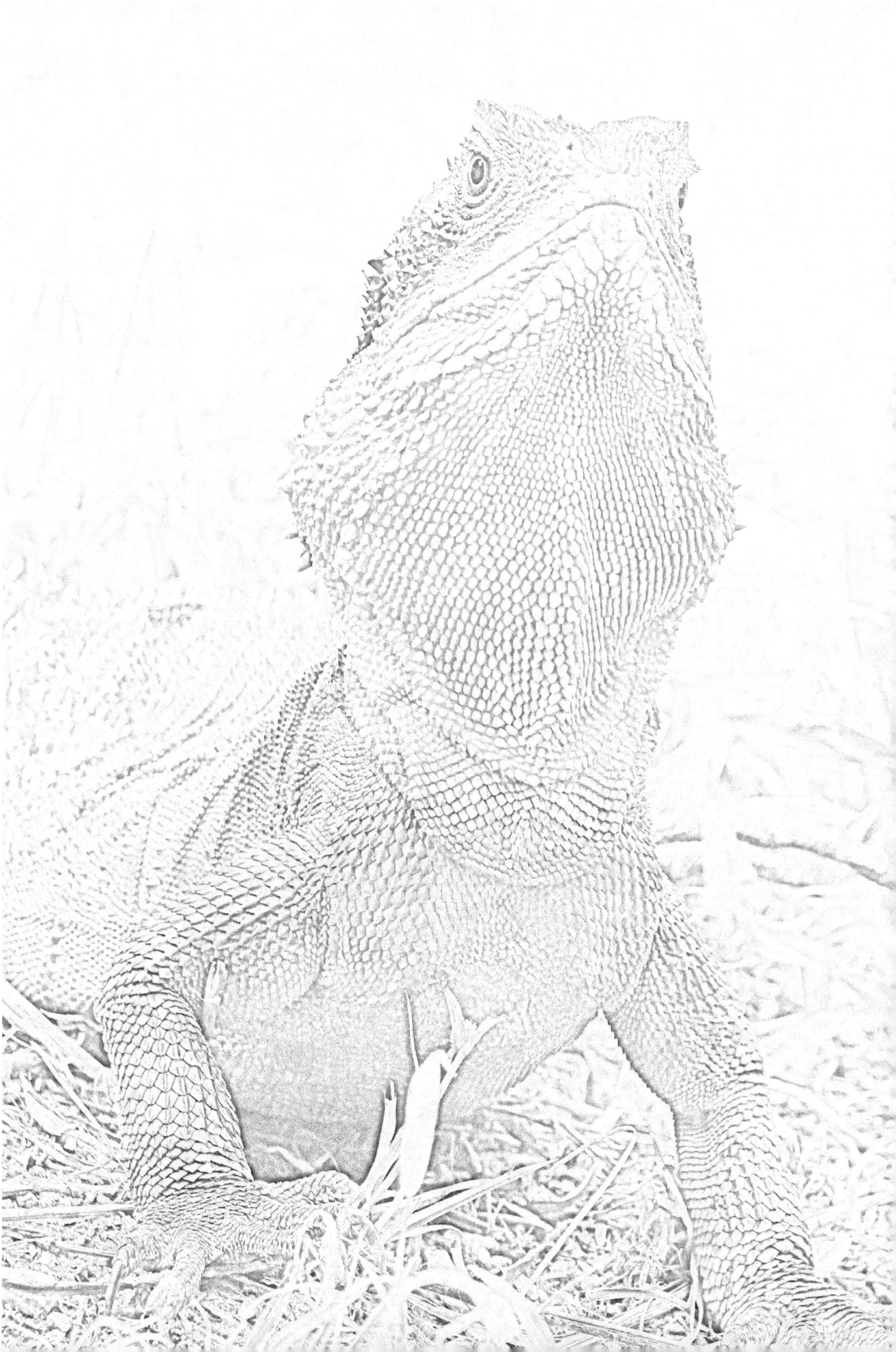

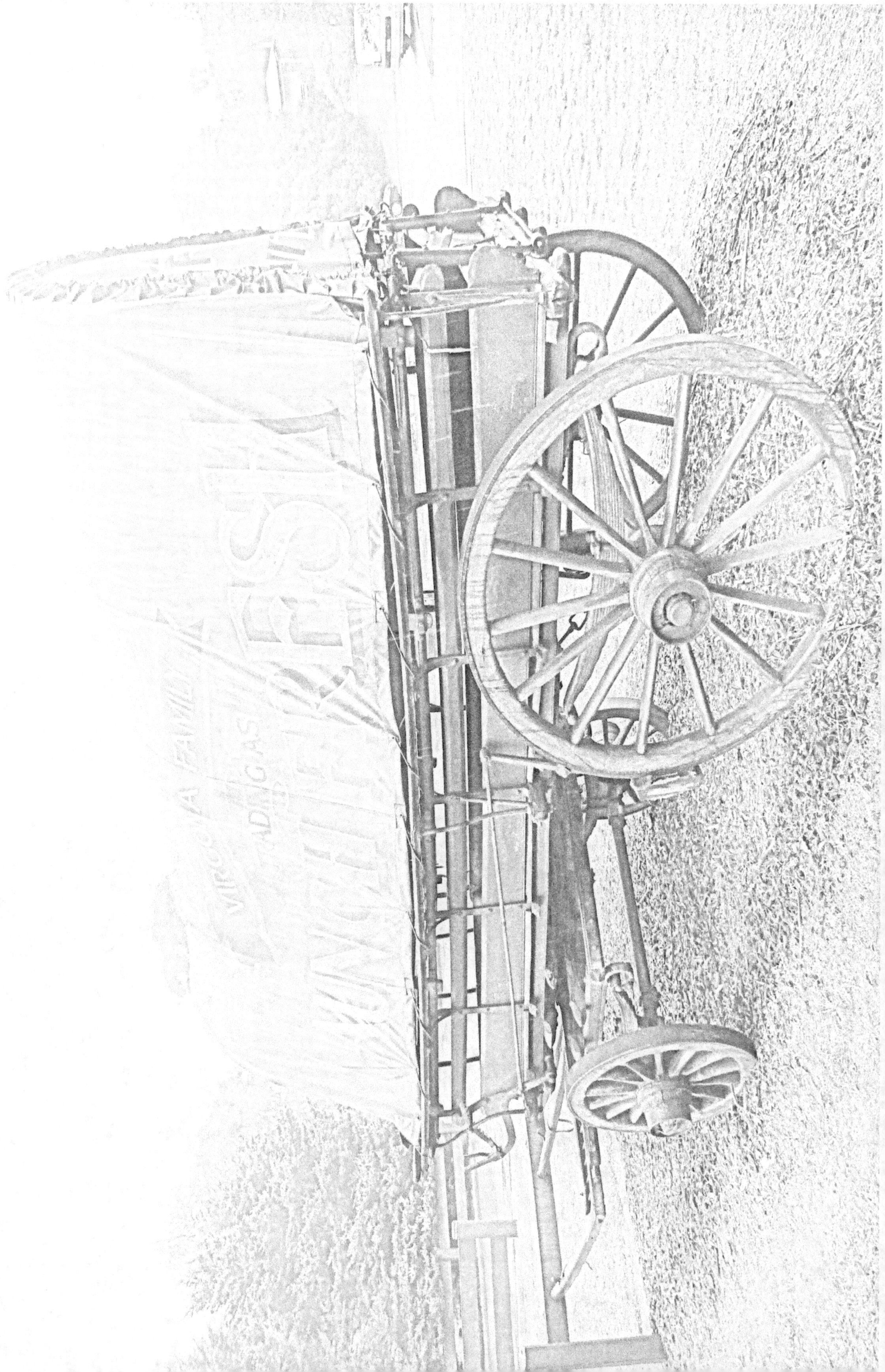

www.ingramcontent.com/pod-product-compliance
Lightning Source LLC
Chambersburg PA
CBHW081050180526
45170CB00005B/1748